A BRIEF HISTORY OF WOMEN

A Play in Four Scenes

by Alan Ayckbourn

SAMUEL FRENCH

ISBN 978-0-573-11670-4

concordtheatricals.co.uk
concordtheatricals.com

FOR AMATEUR PRODUCTION ENQUIRIES

UNITED KINGDOM AND WORLD
EXCLUDING NORTH AMERICA
licensing@concordtheatricals.co.uk

020-7054-7200

Each title is subject to availability from Concord Theatricals,
depending upon country of performance.

USE OF COPYRIGHTED MUSIC

A licence issued by Concord Theatricals to perform this play does not include permission to use the incidental music specified in this publication. In the United Kingdom: Where the place of performance is already licensed by the PERFORMING RIGHT SOCIETY (PRS) a return of the music used must be made to them. If the place of performance is not so licensed then application should be made to PRS for Music (www.prsformusic.com.). A separate and additional licence from PHONOGRAPHIC PERFORMANCE LTD.(www. ppluk. com) may be needed whenever commercial recordings are used. Outside the United Kingdom: Please contact the appropriate music licensing authority in your territory for the rights to any incidental music.

USE OF COPYRIGHTED THIRD-PARTY MATERIALS

Licensees are solely responsible for obtaining formal written permission from copyright owners to use copyrighted third-party materials (e.g., artworks, logos) in the performance of this play and are strongly cautioned to do so. If no such permission is obtained by the licensee, then the licensee must use only original materials that the licensee owns and controls. Licensees are solely responsible and liable for clearances of all third-party copyrighted materials, and shall indemnify the copyright owners of the play(s) and their licensing agent, Concord Theatricals Ltd., against any costs, expenses, losses and liabilities arising from the use of such copyrighted third-party materials by licensees.

IMPORTANT BILLING AND CREDIT REQUIREMENTS

If you have obtained performance rights to this title, please refer to your licensing agreement for important billing and credit requirements.

A BRIEF HISTORY OF WOMEN was first performed at the Stephen Joseph Theatre, Scarborough, on 5 September 2017. The director was Alan Ayckbourn, with design by Kevin Jenkins, and lighting by Jason Taylor. The composer was Simon Slater and the choreographer was Sheila Carter. The cast was as follows:

ANTHONY SPATES . . . . .Antony Eden

**LORD EDWARD KIRKBRIDGE / DR WYN WILLIAMS /
DENNIS DUNBAR / GORDON** . . . . Russell Dixon

**CAPTAIN FERGUS FFLUKE / DESMOND KENNEDY /
RORY TUDOR / JIM SEABOURNE-WATSON** . . . . .Laurence Pears

**LADY CAROLINE KIRKBRIDGE / MISS EVA MILLER /
PAT WRIGGLY / CAROLINE SEABOURNE**. . . . . Frances Marshall

**LADY CYNTHIA / MISS URSULA BROCK /
JENNY TYLER / TILLY SEABOURNE-WATSON** . . . . .Laura Matthews

**MRS REGINALD FFLUKE / MISS PHOEBE LONG /
GILLIAN DUNBAR / RUBY JENSEN** . . . . Louise Shuttleworth

This production was presented with the same cast at 59E59 Theaters, New York, commencing 1 May 2018 as part of the Brits Off Broadway Festival.

CASTING NOTE

A Brief History of Women is written for a cast of six (3 women, 3 men). The suggested (and preferred!) distribution of the twenty-one roles is as follows:

ANTHONY SPATES – aged 17-77

LORD EDWARD KIRKBRIDGE – aged 65
DR WYNFORD WILLIAMS – aged 50
DENNIS DUNBAR – aged 50
GORDON – aged 50

CAPTAIN FERGUS FFLUKE – aged 27
DESMOND KENNEDY – aged 30
RORY TUDOR – aged 27
JIM SEABOURNE-WATSON – aged 30

LADY CAROLINE KIRKBRIDGE – aged 38
MISS EVA MILLER – aged 40
PAT WRIGGLY – aged 40
CAROLINE SEABOURNE – aged 97

LADY CYNTHIA – aged 20
MISS URSULA BROCK – aged 25
JENNY TYLER – aged 22
TILLY SEABOURNE-WATSON – aged 27

MRS REGINALD FFLUKE – aged 50
MISS PHOEBE LONG – aged 45
GILLIAN DUNBAR – aged 45
RUBY JENSEN – aged 40

NOTES ON MUSIC

Required Music

Licensees are provided with piano-vocal sheet music for "You Can Try" on pages 64 & 65 for an additional fee. This music is required for performance.

Suggested Music for Part Three

Whilst there is no requirement to use these pieces, it may be of use to refer to some of the music used in the original production:

"Dawn from the Daphnis et Chloé Suite" by Ravel for the Jack and the Beanstalk "ballet" rehearsals.

Dvorak's "Humanesque" for where Spates and Gillian practice the cow dance.

PART ONE

Kirkbridge Manor 1925

CHARACTERS

ANTHONY SPATES – a footman, aged 17
LORD EDWARD KIRKBRIDGE – aged 65
LADY CAROLINE KIRKBRIDGE – his wife, aged 38
LADY CYNTHIA – their daughter, aged 20
CAPTAIN FERGUS FFLUKE – her fiancé, aged 27
MRS REGINALD FFLUKE – Fergus's mother, aged 50

TIME

An autumn evening.

SETTING

Four separate areas denoting sections of the ground floor of Kirkbridge Manor, including parts of the hall and main staircase, the study, the ballroom and the terrace.

1925. A section of Kirkbridge Manor, a Georgian country house. There are four visible areas, or parts of them:

The main hall extending offstage, the ballroom, also extending offstage, the study and a section of a grand terrace.

Despite the fact that all the dividing walls are invisible and all the doors are mimed, the sound-proofing between the areas is extremely effective, and when our hero and central character, **ANTHONY SPATES,** *moves between them, we hear only what he hears.*

In the ballroom, seated just inside the hall door, are **LADY CAROLINE KIRKBRIDGE,** *thirty-eight, and* **MRS REGINALD FFLUKE,** *fifty. Although they are talking animatedly, we cannot hear what they are saying. Similarly, in the study are seated* **LORD EDWARD KIRKBRIDGE,** *sixty-five, in silent conversation with* **CAPTAIN FERGUS FFLUKE,** *twenty-seven.*

ANTHONY SPATES, *a young footman of seventeen, enters along the hall. He carries a silver tray, upon which is a newly mixed cocktail.*

The sound of bar activity behind him and the muffled sound from the ballroom of a small twenties dance band.*

As he opens the ballroom door, the music increases in volume, mingled with the sound of general activity and

*A licence to produce *A Brief History of Women* does not include a performance licence for any third-party or copyrighted music. Licensees should create an original composition or use music in the public domain. For further information, please see Music Use Note on page iii.

chatter. Most distinctly we hear **LADY KIRKBRIDGE** *and* **MRS REGINALD**'s *voices for the first time.*

LADY K *(in full flow)* ...No, it's my daughter I feel sorry for, that's all. I think it's unforgivable of both of them, behaving like this, unforgivable...

MRS R I don't think you can blame Fergus, my dear, it's hardly my son's fault, is it? It's men, darling, men. They've simply no sense of priorities, have they? I gave up trying to civilise them years ago...

SPATES *(hovering with his tray)* Your drink, milady.

LADY K Thank you, Spates.

> **SPATES** *places the fresh drink beside her and, during the next, gathers up their empties.*

SPATES *(to* **MRS R***)* Would you care for anything else, madam?

MRS R *(straining to hear him over the music)* What? What was that?

SPATES *(speaking louder)* Would you care for another drink, madam?

MRS R I can't hear a word you're saying – do they have to play this music quite so loudly, Caroline? These days they seem to insist on playing everything at this deafening volume. I do blame the Americans, you know. All that terrible jazz music. They'll all be deaf as posts before they're thirty. They never played as loudly as this in our day, surely?

LADY K It is rather loud, I must say.

MRS R Come round to the other side of me, young man. To my good ear.

> **SPATES** *moves round dutifully.*

These people playing, are they Americans?

LADY K No, I booked them locally. I understand they're from Maidenhead.

MRS R Really? I can't believe people actually enjoy this sort of thing in Maidenhead.

LADY K Let's ask Spates, shall we? Spates, you're a young person, do you find this loud, do you?

SPATES The music, milady?

MRS R If you can call it that.

SPATES I find it very – pleasant, milady. Very catchy.

LADY K *(playfully)* Oh, do you? Does it make you want to get up and dance, Spates?

SPATES *(embarrassed)* I wouldn't quite put it like that, milady.

MRS R *(amused)* Oh, I do believe the boy's blushing!

> **LADY CYNTHIA**, *twenty, comes on, straight from the dance floor.*

CYNTHIA *(as she appears)* Mummy!

LADY K Oh, darling! Are you enjoying yourself?

CYNTHIA Mummy, is he coming? Is Fergus coming to join us? Why isn't he here? Fergus should be here, as well. It's only me there.

LADY K He's coming, darling. He's talking to Edward in the study. He'll be here soon, I promise.

CYNTHIA I'm running out of people to dance with. Everyone's starting to stare at me...

LADY K No, they're not, darling, they're really not! That's only your imagination.

CYNTHIA ..."Oh, look, she's all on her own, poor girl, at her own engagement party! Where's her fiancé, do you think? He must have broken it off?"

MRS R Nonsense! Now don't be so silly –

LADY K That's not what they're saying at all, darling –

CYNTHIA They are!

LADY K – everyone's far too busy enjoying themselves.

CYNTHIA *(as she goes)* I'll soon be left dancing with the servants, at this rate...

She goes off again.

LADY K *(calling after her)* You can always dance with Spates, here, darling!

MRS R Caroline, honestly –!

LADY K I'm sure you're secretly a wonderful dancer, aren't you, Spates?

MRS R My dear! So familiar!

LADY K How do you mean?

MRS R With the servants. You mustn't be quite so familiar. You'll be giving the boy ideas, far above his station.

LADY K What rubbish! Come along, Rowena, do have another drink. Max mixes the best cocktails. You must have one of these. What's this called again, Spates?

SPATES A Bee's Knees, milady.

LADY K A Bee's Knees.

MRS R Heavens! What's a Bee's Knees?

LADY K It's from America. They drink it in speakeasies, apparently.

MRS R What on earth's in it?

LADY K Mostly gin, a fearful lot of gin. They're really rather addictive, I must say. Delicious. It was an excellent recommendation, Spates.

SPATES Thank you, milady.

MRS R Well, maybe I ought to try one, then.

LADY K I warn you, you'll end up wanting more of them. Are you still keeping tally, Spates? Still keeping count, are you?

I asked him to keep a tally of how many I'd had. How many so far, Spates?

SPATES Six, milady.

MRS R *squawks with laughter.*

LADY K Six! This can't be my sixth, surely?

SPATES No, that's your seventh, milady.

MRS R Caroline, really, Caroline, darling! You're incorrigible!

LADY K It's never my seventh! I have not had six of these already, that's ridiculous!

MRS R Caroline, you've been tossing them down like water, dear, all evening!

LADY K Then this is definitely my last! This is positively the last drink of the night for me. No more after this! Spates, if I ask for another, you are to say firmly, "No, milady, you have had quite enough!" Do you understand?

SPATES Yes, milady. One Bee's Knees for you, madam.

LADY K And, Spates, before you do anything else, please go into the study, and tell them Lady Kirkbridge says if Captain ffluke neglects my daughter any longer, he will find she has run off with some attractive ruffian from the village.

MRS R I wouldn't at all blame her if she did.

SPATES *(starting to leave with his tray)* Very good, milady. Madam.

MRS R *(staring at* SPATES *as he goes, to* LADY K*)* I must say, he's rather dishy. Where did you find that one?

LADY K Spates? He's local. Helps out occasionally. Farming family.

MRS R We plough the fields and scatter, what?

She laughs loudly.

SPATES *leaves the ballroom, closing the door behind him. The sounds there reduce sharply and are replaced by the hall sounds as before.*

He crosses the hall with his tray with the empty glasses and goes out to the bar.

He returns, almost at once, his tray empty, and moves to the study door, where he pauses and knocks discreetly.

LORD K *(from within, faintly)* Come!

SPATES enters the study and hovers, waiting for a suitable gap in the conversation.

(in full flow) ...No, as I say, as soon as I've popped my clogs, this whole caboosh, this entire estate, according to my father's will, technically passes to my younger brother, William...

FERGUS Oh, I see, not to Lady Kirkbridge?

LORD K Not as things stand at present. Not unless I choose to will it to her. *(smiling)* Which I haven't, as yet. Currently, I'm happy to let things stand, maintain the status quo. Once you get to my age, Fergus, you'll find your nearest and dearest grow progressively more interested in the state of your health. Caroline's my third wife, younger than me by thirty years and, don't misunderstand me, I'm very fond of her, as a wife, she's certainly a great deal more than adequate. But I've absolutely no illusions as to why she married me. None at all. Her overriding intention was to get her claws securely fastened into the Kirkbridge cash flow. I don't delude myself she married me for my virile manly physique, old boy. My late father's words, with regards to women, still ring in my ears: Love 'em, if you have to, bed 'em, if you want to, but trust 'em at your peril. *(irritably, to SPATES)* Yes, what is it, boy? Hovering there...?

SPATES Excuse me, milord, Lady Kirkbridge was wondering whether you'd care to join her and Mrs ffluke in the ballroom?

LORD K No, we bloody well wouldn't! Tell Lady Kirkbridge, Captain ffluke and I haven't yet finished our conversation. We will join them when we are ready to join them and not before. Is that, clear, boy? Don't bother us again! Now, there's a shining example of what I was saying, Fergus. Give women an inch of rope and before you know it they've formed a lynch mob. Fatal! The moment they got the vote, they expect us to start treating them as bloody equals. Well, they're not equals, not at all, not in my book. Medically speaking they're an entirely separate, inferior species. Smaller brains, far less muscle. First, they're given the vote, what the hell's next? I'll tell you what comes next. Socialism. That's what comes next. Followed closely by Armageddon, mark my words. All I can say is, thank God I won't be around to see it. I'll be long gone by then. *(to* **SPATES***)* Well, don't just stand there like a wet Tuesday, boy, make yourself useful and fetch us a couple more brandies.

SPATES Yes, milord.

During the next, **SPATES** *locates and gathers up their empty glasses.*

LORD K I'll have you know, that Captain ffluke here is a national hero.

FERGUS *(modestly, shrugging)* Well, hardly that...

LORD K Ever met a national hero before, have you, boy? In the flesh?

SPATES No, milord.

LORD K Well, you're looking at one now, boy. Much decorated man, this one. Risked his life for the rest of us, so that we could sleep peacefully in our beds. Military Medal. Royal Army Medical Corps. Acts of gallantry and devotion to duty under fire. What do you make of that, boy?

SPATES Congratulations, sir.

LORD K Now, fetch him a bloody drink. He's earned one.

FERGUS *(hesitantly)* Well, perhaps just one more. Then I must, really...

LORD K Now, getting back to my brother William – generally known to the family as Mad Willie – Mad, Bad Willie – the chances are, he won't even bother to lay claim to the estate, even if he's offered it. He's gone and joined up with this new Labour Party.

FERGUS Oh, has he? Has he? That's interesting.

LORD K *Interesting?* Complete bloody lunacy! Fancy calling themselves the *"Labour"* Party, for God's sake! More or less implying that the rest of us never do a stroke of work, eh?

He and **FERGUS** *laugh.*

SPATES *goes out, closing the door behind him and cutting off their voices. Bar noises return. He returns there with the empty glasses. He re-enters with his tray, which now has the cocktail intended for* **MRS R.**

He returns to the ballroom. The music again increases in volume as he opens the door.

LADY K *(still in full flow)* ...No, I'm sorry, Rowena, I don't agree with you. Not at all. I think these class differentiations belong in the last century, I really do. Since the war, we're all surely much more equal than we ever were before. I mean they actually fought side by side, didn't they? As equals under fire...

MRS R My dear, if you don't mind my saying so, you're beginning to sound most appallingly liberal...

LADY K Well, what if I am? I don't care...

MRS R All I'm saying is that, in a perfect world, everyone should know their place and stay there. That's all I was saying –

LADY K I fear for our future, Rowena, I really do. If we stick with the old values as they were, well, just witness what happened in Russia, my dear –

A licence to produce A Brief History of Women *does not include a performance licence for any third-party or copyrighted music. Licensees should create an original composition or use music in the public domain. For further information, please see Music Use Note on page iii.*

MRS R Dear God, don't even mention the Russians!

LADY K I mean, I worry for Cynthia. She has her whole life ahead of her. I worry dreadfully for her, Rowena. For any young person, growing up these days, come to that. Life, just at present, is simply a huge question mark. Everything's so in the melting pot, don't you feel?

SPATES *(placing the glass beside* **MRS R***)* Your Bee's Knees, madam.

> *He remains within earshot through the next, watching the offstage dancers.*

MRS R I think you're worrying unnecessarily, Caroline. I know she's only a stepdaughter but your husband must have made some sort of provision for her, hasn't he? She surely has no need to worry?

LADY K I don't think he has made provision. Not yet, at any rate.

MRS R What are you saying? He hasn't allowed for her? But doesn't that...?

LADY K No, not for either of us. He keeps – putting it off. As things stand at present, everything, this house, the whole estate goes to his brother, William.

MRS R Oh, dear God! So you'll get nothing? Either of you?

LADY K Not at present, no. Not unless he alters things. But I'm sure it's just a matter of time before he does...

MRS R This is extraordinary. Why on earth did you agree to marry him, dear girl, in the first place?

LADY K *(rather lamely)* I thought I – I convinced myself, at the time, I was in love with him –

MRS R Well, that's no reason at all to get married, is it?

LADY K – and I had the impression that he loved me, as well.

MRS R That's even less reason.

LADY K Now I'm not quite so sure...

MRS R Whether you love him?

LADY K No.

MRS R Or whether he loves you?

LADY K No.

MRS R I think, if I may say so, Caroline, that you've been unbelievably naïve. Almost to the point of downright stupidity. Take my advice, dear, and get him to write you into that will *tout de suite.*

LADY K *(unhappily)* I sometimes think he doesn't give a jot what happens to either of us. He says, you never have to worry about women, they always cope, somehow. They can always manage to scrape by, find some luckless man to sponge off.

MRS R What an appalling thing to say! That's so Victorian!

LADY K Well, he is, darling, if he had his way, he'd have us all back in corsets and crinolines. I keep saying, Edward, this is the twentieth century, my dear...

   CYNTHIA *returns briefly.*

CYNTHIA *(despairingly)* Mummy, please...

   And she goes off again.

LADY K *(after her)* Yes, darling! *(suddenly, agitated)* Spates, did you find Captain ffluke?

SPATES Yes, milady.

LADY K Did you tell him we need him here? Urgently?

SPATES Yes, milady.

LADY K And are they coming?

SPATES *(hesitantly)* I'm – not entirely sure, milady.

LADY K If they're not here within two minutes, I'm going to become very angry. You tell them that from me!

SPATES *(moving nervously away)* Yes, milady.

LADY K Very angry indeed!

MRS R Caroline, steady, dear...

SPATES *(hurriedly leaving the ballroom)* Yes, milady.

LADY K No, hell with them both, Rowena. I'm sorry, I know he's your son, but to hell with them. Wretched men! I've had it up to here with them! I spent months arranging all this, you know –

> **SPATES** *closes the door behind him, cutting her off. The scene continues silently as he hurries across the hall to the study door. He is about to knock when he remembers the drinks that had been ordered. He hurries back to the bar and returns almost at once with two fresh brandies on his tray. He knocks on the study door.*

LORD K *(from within as before, faintly)* Come!

> **SPATES** *enters the study, closing the door behind him.*

(in full flow as before) ...And I have to tell you, Fergus, old chap, that bloke Ramsay MacDonald terrifies the life out of me. Give a chap like that one sniff of power, let him get his hands on the ship of state's tiller, we're all heading for the rocks, old boy, I can tell you. Women and children first, all hands on deck, every man for himself.

FERGUS *(getting rather depressed from what he's hearing)* Yes... Yes...

LORD K Well, I'm out of it soon enough. Best of luck to you.

FERGUS Thank you.

LORD K You're going to need it. *(seeing SPATES)* Ah, at last! Gunga Din. Where the blazes did you get to? We're both dying of thirst here, man.

SPATES I'm sorry, milord. I got – delayed.

LORD K Delayed?

SPATES Yes, milord.

LORD K You sound like a blasted railway engine.

SPATES Lady Kirkbridge is becoming somewhat – anxious – that you join her, milord, that's all –

FERGUS *(rising nervously)* Yes, well perhaps we'd better, perhaps –

LORD K You tell Lady Kirkbridge, Spates, that I'm not in the habit of being treated like some piddling little lap dog! Expected to run around at her beck and call.

SPATES Yes, milord.

LORD K Fergus, sit down!

> **FERGUS** *sits.*
>
> *(to* **SPATES***)* And you, get out!

SPATES Yes, milord.

LORD K We're both going to enjoy our brandy and finish our conversation, like civilised men. In a couple of months' time, you'll be my son-in-law, Fergus, and I'm entrusting you with my stepdaughter. I'm handing you her reins. You needn't worry, she'll come with a dowry, I'll see to that, but I'll leave them to sweat it out for a bit longer. If the girl's anything like her mother – and she came as part of the package when I married Caroline – if she's anything like her mother, you may find, to start out with, she's a little bit frisky. Headstrong. She may need a bit of breaking in. A firmer hand. A touch of the crop. But nothing, I'm sure, that a war hero like yourself can't handle, once you've got the bridle on her –

> **SPATES** *creeps out, closing the door behind him and cutting off further conversation, which continues silently under the next.*
>
> *He stands in the hall for a moment, taking a series of deep breaths to calm himself.*
>
> *He prepares to enter the ballroom again.*

As he opens the door, **LADY K** *has now rather worked herself up to a new level.*

LADY K *(in full despairing flow)* ...I've been left to do everything! Everything!

MRS R *(very concerned)* Caroline, dear...

LADY K Sending out hundreds of invitations, organising the servants, the kitchens, the garden staff for the flowers, arranging to have these windows cleaned by an exorbitant specialist firm, booking that wretched band. I even had this ballroom floor specially re-polished! I was left to do everything! And what thanks do I get? From anyone?

CYNTHIA *returns.*

CYNTHIA *(impatiently pleading)* Mummy, please! Please! Please...

LADY K *(irritably, barking at her)* Oh, for goodness' sake, Cynthia, just a moment, will you!

MRS R *(nervously sensing her state)* Caroline, dear...

LADY K No, honestly, it's all too much! It's just too much!

She rises and stumbles to the door, nearly losing her balance. **SPATES** *steps forward to assist her.*

(shrugging him off) Don't touch me!

SPATES *steps back, standing helplessly by.*

CYNTHIA Mummy? Is something wrong? Mummy!

LADY K I'm going to talk to both of them. They can't treat us like this!

CYNTHIA *(puzzled)* Mummy?

MRS R It's all right, Cynthia, your mother's just a little... *(calling after* **LADY K***)* Caroline, dear!

LADY K *staggers into the hall. She is rather drunk. She starts to weave her way towards the study.* **SPATES** *follows*

*her cautiously, at a distance, closing the door behind
them and remaining ready to catch her.*

MRS R, *during the next, gently walks with* **CYNTHIA**
back onto the dance floor. They exit.

LADY K *(arriving at the study door, to* **SPATES***)* They're still in
here, you say?

SPATES Yes, milady, but I really wouldn't advise –

Before he can finish, she bursts into the room.

SPATES *follows her tentatively.*

LADY K *(as she enters, angrily)* Edward, are you joining us or not?

LORD K *(startled)* What the hell –?

LADY K Are you both proposing to spend the entire evening in
here, because if so –

LORD K *(livid)* How dare you come bursting in here! We're
having a private conversation, get out at once! You know
you're not allowed in my study, I never allow women in my
study, now get out, do you hear me?

LADY K *(equally angrily)* Edward, if you do not come into the
ballroom this moment, I'm cancelling this party and sending
everyone home, including the band –

LORD K I don't care if you do! Go ahead, see if I care! Go on,
cancel your piddling little party! Who cares? Now, get out
immediately, you know you're not allowed in here, we're in
the middle of a private conversation. Bugger off!

FERGUS, *alarmed by this exchange, backs apprehensively
to the terrace doorway.*

FERGUS *(tentatively)* Well, I think I'd better be going, if you'll
excuse me...

*He goes out onto the terrace without the others noticing.
During the next, he makes his way across the terrace and*

*through the door to the ballroom. He crosses the floor
and goes off, presumably to join his fiancée.*

LADY K *(over this)* You really are quite the most despicable
man, aren't you? You're inconsiderate, rude, you have the
manners of a rutting pig –

LORD K Oh, shut up, you're drunk woman –

LADY K – an insensitive, charmless, humourless boor –

LORD K – disgustingly drunk. Look at you, you can hardly
stand up, can you –?

LADY K – with not a single thought, a scrap of consideration
for anyone other than yourself. You're a selfish, biased,
snobbish bigot –

LORD K If you don't get out this minute, I warn you, I'll have
you thrown out, you drunken slut –

LADY K – a mannerless misanthropic oaf! You're hell to live with!
A total bully. Making life utterly miserable for everybody –

LORD K Well, if you're that bloody miserable, why don't you leave,
woman? Go on, get out! And take that appalling spoilt brat
with you, while you're at it! She's a pain in the backside, as
well, ghastly snivelling child!

LADY K *(stung by this last)* How dare you say that about my
daughter, how dare you?

LORD K She ought to be put down. God knows where its father
came from, probably out of a circus –

LADY K You know perfectly well, he was a highly successful
businessman. At least he worked for a living, unlike some
people I can mention...

LORD K *(sneering)* Businessman? He was a tradesman, a bloody
jumped-up little shopkeeper, that's all he was...

LADY K You're a fine one to look down your nose. At least he was
a proper man. At least he was capable of having children.

LORD K *(his turn to be stung)* What exactly do you mean by that?

LADY K I hate to remind you, dear husband, in order to have children, you have to do something about it as well. Call yourself a husband? I hardly ever see you. You shut yourself away in here all day. That's when you're not out slaughtering innocent wildlife. And, as for the night times, what sort of life is it for me, do you imagine? Night after night, all on my own in that vast double bed...

LORD K Perhaps if you made a bit more of an effort, I might get the urge to join you. You're like a bloody limp lettuce, most of the time. Lying there on our wedding night with your eyes closed, your knees clamped together, with about as much allure as a dish of cold porridge –

LADY K That was probably because you'd just vomited, over my new nightdress. You came to bed roaring drunk and proceeded to be violently sick all down me – How deeply romantic, that was! No, if truth be told, dearest, I suspect you're not that way inclined, are you? Women don't really interest you, do they? You're much happier with a dog or another jolly good chap. In all honesty, I think you're probably a homosexual. A queer. I think you must be a queer.

LORD K is silent for a moment as though absorbing this ultimate insult to his manhood.

He appears to be undergoing some sort of internal explosion.

LORD K *(speaking with difficulty)* Don't...you...ever...call...me... that...again!

LADY K *(realising she's gone too far)* I'm sorry. I didn't mean that...

LORD K You insolent – common little jumped-up tart... You... You... You... Socialist!

He lunges at her. She retreats, raising her arms to protect her face. He keeps advancing, driving her into a corner.

LADY K *(as she does so)* Go on, then! Go on! Hit me. That's what you usually do, isn't it? Go on, if it makes you feel any better, hitting a woman, you fairy!

With a final roar of fury, **LORD K** *raises his arm to strike her.*

SPATES, *who has stood throughout this, unnoticed and pressed against the wall in apparent frozen horror, is suddenly galvanised into action. He steps forward and grasps* **LORD K***'s raised arm.*

LORD K *(startled)* What the hell –? What do you think you're doing, man?

SPATES I'm sorry, milord, I can't allow this, I really can't...

LORD K *(struggling)* What are you doing? Let go of me at once, do you hear?

SPATES *(still holding on to him)* I'm so sorry, I'm terribly sorry, milord...

LORD K *(still struggling to free himself)* Let go! How dare you! How dare you manhandle me, you lout!

He tries to hit **SPATES** *with his free hand, but* **SPATES** *catches that arm, too, before it can make contact.*

SPATES, *facing him now, holds both his arms which, as* **LORD K** *struggles, are gradually extended sideways to their full extent, leaving both men's faces literally inches from each other.*

LORD K *struggles apoplectically, but* **SPATES,** *younger and fitter, manages to restrain him without too much difficulty.*

SPATES *walks* **LORD K** *backwards towards the desk chair.* **LADY K,** *meantime, manages to slither sideways to a place of safety.*

LORD K *(twisting impotently)* You'll pay for this, boy! By God you'll pay for this, you riff-raff! I'll have you horsewhipped, you hear? Horsewhipped to within an inch of your worthless little life! I'll make you rue the very day you were born, you oaf! You thug! How dare you! Let go of me!

SPATES *(under this last, apologetically)* I'm so sorry, milord, I'm really sorry. I can't allow you to do that, milord, I simply can't! I'm so sorry, I really am sorry, milord...

As they near the chair, **LORD K** *appears to be having difficulty breathing or speaking, displaying early signs of a heart attack.*

LADY K *(becoming aware of this)* Spates! Spates, I think you ought to let it go now. I think you should release my husband, please? Spates, let go now! Let go! *(sharply)* Let go!

SPATES *(abruptly doing so)* Yes, milady.

LORD K *slumps into the chair, still fighting for breath.*

LADY K Thank you, Spates.

SPATES Thank you, milady. I'm so sorry, milady.

LADY K Yes. I'm sorry, too, that you were – that you had to – witness all that. I do apologise. You never should have had to listen to that. It was quite unforgivable of both of us.

SPATES *(clearly shaken by what he has seen)* Did he –? Did he really hit you, milady? Has he actually hit you? Really?

LADY K Oh, yes. Quite regularly. I'm amazed you didn't know. Most of the servants know. I believe it's quite common knowledge below stairs.

SPATES I'm only part-time, milady. Only temporary.

LADY K It's fairly run-of-the-mill marital behaviour, in our circles. More prevalent than you imagine. I take it your father never strikes your mother?

SPATES No, milady. She'd have hit him straight back. She packs a fair wallop, my mum.

LADY K I'm delighted to hear it. But then I'm sure life is much more civilised, down on the farm.

LORD K *is starting to wheeze rather alarmingly. They look at him.*

(somewhat detached) I think we may need to get someone to look at him, you know.

SPATES I'll fetch someone, milady.

He moves to the door and goes into the hall. As he does so, CYNTHIA *and* FERGUS *appear in the ballroom, followed by* MRS R. *The band is still playing.*

(urgently) Excuse me, Captain.

FERGUS Yes, what is it, man?

SPATES It's milord – he's – it seems – it seems he's had some sort of a seizure –

FERGUS What did you say? A seizure, you say?

SPATES It seems to be a sort of seizure –

CYNTHIA Oh, God, a seizure?

MRS R What's the boy saying? Has someone had a seizure?

FERGUS How do you know it's a seizure?

CYNTHIA A seizure!

SPATES It has all the signs of a seizure, sir.

MRS R Who's he saying's had a seizure?

SPATES We think it's a seizure, sir. We're almost certain it's a seizure.

FERGUS Let me see. I'll soon see if it's a seizure. Stand aside!

He brushes SPATES *aside and goes into the study.* CYNTHIA *and* MRS R *follow him.*

SPATES *brings up the rear.*

LORD K is still wheezing in the chair while LADY K *watches him, seemingly indifferent.*

FERGUS *(seeing him, concerned)* Oh, my God!

CYNTHIA *(simultaneously)* Oh, no!

MRS R *(simultaneously)* Oh, heavens!

FERGUS *(immediately taking charge)* Stand well back, everyone, this looks serious. Let me take a look!

He steps forward to examine LORD K *and does so during the next.*

CYNTHIA Mummy, are you all right?

LADY K Yes, I'm perfectly all right, darling.

MRS R Are you quite sure, Caroline? What on earth happened?

LADY K I've no idea. We were just sitting here quietly, Edward and I, and he just suddenly exploded.

MRS R Exploded?

LADY K Yes, he simply blew up. All of a sudden. Just like he is now.

CYNTHIA How can someone blow up? How can that possibly happen?

LADY K *(shrugging)* Well, you know your father, darling, he was always threatening to do that, wasn't he? I think it finally happened. You were here with us, Spates, that's how it was, wasn't it?

SPATES *(tactfully)* Very much that way, milady.

FERGUS He's had a slight heart attack, from the look of it. We must get him to lie down, he needs to lie down. If he sits any longer like this, he'll choke to death. *(to* SPATES*)* Here, you, give me a hand with him!

SPATES Yes, Captain.

He and SPATES *lever* LORD K *out of the chair, with difficulty.* LORD K *makes strangulated vocal sounds.*

FERGUS *(as they do so)* Easy with him! Easy there!

MRS R What's that he's saying? What's he trying to say?

FERGUS *(straining to hear)* It sounds like "little bastard." *(laughing)* I hope he isn't referring to me!

CYNTHIA Careful, now!

MRS R Careful with him.

FERGUS We must get him to the bedroom, loosen his clothing. So I can examine him properly.

They half-carry LORD K *to the foot of the stairs.* FERGUS *and* SPATES *lift him up with difficulty, stair by stair.*

CYNTHIA *and* MRS R *follow on.*

MRS R *(turning back, as they leave)* Caroline, are you coming up?

LADY K *(still seated)* No, I just need to sit here quietly, if you don't mind.

MRS R *(sympathetically)* Yes, get over the shock. You do that, dear.

They all go off upstairs, leaving LADY K *sitting alone in the study. Since* SPATES *is no longer in evidence, there is a silence until he finally returns downstairs.*

He reaches the hall, where we can still hear faint sounds from the offstage bar.

SPATES *deliberates before returning to the study. He enters, closing the door. A silence between them.*

LADY K *(eventually)* It wasn't your fault, you know. You're in no way to blame. You mustn't blame yourself in any way. It would probably have happened to him, sooner or later, in any case. The amount he used to eat. His constant drinking.

SPATES *remains silent.*

LADY K Anyway, thank you. I think that time he might really have hurt me. I certainly made him angry enough. It was entirely my fault. I went far too far. I should never have called him a fairy. He held extremely strong views on homosexuality. Much of it involving hanging and horsewhips. Never mind, when he recovers – and knowing him he's bound to, he has the constitution of an ox – he'll doubtless exact his revenge on both of us. Probably by beating me and dismissing you.

Silence.

I'm really sorry if I cost you your job, Spates, I really am. You're very good at it, you know. For a part-timer. You don't deserve to be sacked, Spates. You truly don't. I shall miss you very much. You're practically the only servant we have who's civil to me. Who doesn't snigger behind my back. They all know instinctively, you see, that I'm not quite "pukka," not the real thing. Unlike my blue-blooded predecessor, the late Lady Kirkbridge. They could all tell at a glance, something about me, that told them, underneath, I was a common little shopkeeper's daughter. Something to do with the way I spoke or walked or just simply stood there. A lack of inner self-confidence.

SPATES *(softly)* You're a lady to me, milady. Always have been.

LADY K *(touched)* Thank you, Spates. That means a lot, it really does. Look, I really can't keep calling you Spates, can I? Do you have another name? A Christian name perhaps? That I could use when we're alone?

SPATES Anthony, milady. Though only my mum calls me that. Everyone else calls me Tony.

LADY K All right. Though I'm nearly old enough to be your mother, if you don't object, I'll call you Tony, along with everyone else.

SPATES I'd be honoured, milady.

LADY K Caroline. When we're alone. During the few days we have left before my husband recovers his strength, Caroline. All right?

SPATES *(swallowing nervously)* Yes, milady.

LADY K Say it, then. Caroline.

SPATES *(with difficulty)* Caroline.

> **LADY K** *smiles at him. He smiles back, rather shyly.*

LADY K Do you find me beautiful, Tony? Do you think I'm attractive?

SPATES Very beautiful, milady – Caroline. You're probably the most beautiful woman I know.

LADY K Thank you, Tony.

SPATES And that includes Violet Washburn.

LADY K *(mildly amused)* I'm flattered. Is this Violet Washburn very attractive, then? I don't believe I know her?

SPATES From the village. She's a stunner. But not a patch on you.

> **MRS R** *and* **CYNTHIA** *start returning downstairs.*

> *They are both grim-faced, the latter even a little tearful. They pause briefly in the hall to engage in brief silent discussion, which results in* **CYNTHIA** *going off into the ballroom, while* **MRS R** *moves to the study.*

LADY K Tell me, Tony, have you ever kissed Violet Washburn?

SPATES No, never managed it.

LADY K But you'd liked to have done, I'm sure?

SPATES Given the opportunity, yes, I certainly would.

LADY K Would you like to kiss me, Tony? Given the opportunity?

SPATES *(losing his voice again)* I certainly would – Caroline. Given the opportunity...

LADY K *(smiling)* Well. Opportunity knocks, Tony. Come here.

> SPATES *moves closer to her, but before they have a chance to touch,* MRS R *enters the study. They break apart abruptly.* MRS R *is aware she is interrupting something but is not sure what it is.*

MRS R Sorry. Caroline, we've decided we're going to have to stop the party. Cynthia's in the ballroom, telling everyone to go home. Including the band. Under the circumstances, we can't go on with it, we really can't. I'm sorry to tell you, he's just had a second attack, more serious than the first one. Fergus is doing his best but there really isn't anything he can do. I think you must prepare yourself for the worst.

LADY K *(flatly)* Oh, well. Oh, dear. Well. That's that, then, isn't it?

MRS R It must be such a shock for you. We've had them telephone the hospital but poor Fergus, he didn't even bring his medical bag.

LADY K No, it wouldn't really have been appropriate, would it? Not to his own engagement party.

MRS R Oh, yes, regarding that, Caroline. I think, in the light of recent events, perhaps we might do well to reconsider our future course of action, don't you feel? Jointly? All of us? Frankly and honestly? I mean, circumstances are going to be very different from now on, aren't they? For everyone? Frankly?

> LADY K *smiles and shakes her head.*

(awkwardly) Yes. I think I'd – I'd better get on with – seeing – people off. And so on. You're sure you'll be all right?

LADY K Yes, thank you.

MRS R You're quite sure, now? I wouldn't want to...

LADY K No. Thank you. Off you go, Rowena. Run along, then.

> MRS R *leaves awkwardly. She goes into the ballroom.*

(smiling) She didn't waste any time, did she? Poisonous woman. If I'm honest, I never really cared for her.

SPATES I – didn't quite follow that, I'm afraid.

LADY K No, you wouldn't have done, Tony. You need to know the code, you see. The secret social code. You'll learn it in time, if needs be. Pray God you'll never have to. You'll never have the need to move in such stifling, small-minded, selfish circles of snobbery, not in your lifetime.

SPATES Right. *(slight pause)* I still don't understand.

LADY K You're going to have a much brighter future than that, I'm sure. Have you plans for your future, at all? Are you going to carry on the family tradition on the farm?

SPATES I'm not quite sure what I want to do. All I wanted to do was to better myself, that's why I took the job here. But now...not sure, really. *(shrugging)* Don't know.

LADY K But you still feel the need to better yourself?

SPATES I just can't see a way forward. Not at the moment.

LADY K Have you considered the possibility of getting a bit more education? You're intelligent and bright. You might well benefit from taking things a little further.

SPATES Education? No, I've finished with school, thank you. Don't fancy more of that –

LADY K No, I meant some sort of higher education. Had you considered that?

SPATES Higher education? What's that, then?

LADY K Some sort of college possibly? Maybe even university, who knows?

SPATES *(laughing)* University? Me? What would I be doing, going to a university? Can't you just see that? Couldn't afford it anyway.

LADY K Why not? Things are changing, Tony. We're living in times of change, where everything is altering. Everything.

All around us. Now that we're through that terrible war, the future's bright, my dear. I truly believe that. It's especially bright for young people like yourself. The ones with this whole twentieth century stretching out before them. "The old order changeth, yielding place to new, and God fulfils Himself in many ways."

SPATES That's nice. You make that up yourself, did you?

LADY K *(smiling)* I'm afraid not. Alfred Lord Tennyson.

SPATES Oh. Maybe that's something I'll get to learn at university, eh?

LADY K Perhaps I can pull a few strings, you know. I think we might be due shortly for a visit from mad brother-in-law, William. He sounds as though he might be sympathetic. He may see you as a worthy cause, who can tell?

SPATES As my dad says, you can always dream. Dreams come free. Only things that are, though. Everything else you pays for, sooner or later. *(moving towards the terrace door)* I must be off home.

During the next, **CYNTHIA** *comes from the ballroom and crosses the hall.*

LADY K *(puzzled)* Home?

SPATES I don't live in, you know, I'm only part-time. *(removing his waistcoat)* Mind if I leave this behind? I doubt I'll be needing it again.

LADY K No?

SPATES I don't think I'll be coming back any time soon. Not after that.

LADY K Why? Why can't you? Nobody knows. Nobody saw what happened. I certainly won't say a word.

SPATES *shakes his head.*

You won't be coming back, then? Ever? What, never again?

SPATES If you need to contact me, ask the housekeeper. Mrs Jackson's got my address. Our farm's not too far away.

He steps out onto the terrace.

As he does so, CYNTHIA *enters the study.*

CYNTHIA *(as she enters)* Mummy, it's all been the most horrid evening, simply horrid... Nothing's gone right. And then he has to die on us! Why did he have to die this evening? He's gone and spoilt everything again! Like he always does.

LADY K *(moving to follow* SPATES, *abstractedly)* I'm sure he didn't plan it deliberately, darling. Just a moment...

CYNTHIA *(absorbed in her own grief)* ...Now, everyone's gone home! We've had to cancel my party... I never even got my ring...

LADY K *(stepping onto the terrace)* Just a moment, darling, please. I'll be with you in a minute. *(calling)* Tony! Anthony!

SPATES, *startled, returns to her.*

(to CYNTHIA*)* I just want to say goodbye to Tony.

CYNTHIA To who? Say goodbye to who? *(seeing who it is)* Oh, him. Why on earth are you saying goodbye to him?

LADY K *(ignoring her, to* SPATES*)* Are you quite sure you've never once had a kiss from Violet Washburn?

SPATES *(confused)* What?

LADY K She's never kissed you, even once?

SPATES Never.

LADY K Do you swear?

SPATES I swear, never...

LADY K Well so long as I'm the first...

She grasps his head and pulls him into a long, deep kiss.

CYNTHIA *watches, thunderstruck, her mouth open.*

CYNTHIA *(a silent scream)* Mummy!

LADY K *finally breaks away. They are both somewhat breathless, particularly the startled* **SPATES**.

LADY K Goodbye, Tony.

SPATES *(faintly)* Goodbye, milady...

He staggers off along the terrace, still slightly weak at the knees. It was probably as good an experience as he could ever have had from Violet Washburn.

CYNTHIA *(recovering, outraged, shrilly)* Mummy, how *could* you? How simply *could* you? He's a *servant*! How could you kiss a *servant*? How could you possibly...?

As **SPATES** *moves away and out of earshot, smiling,* **CYNTHIA**'s *voice gradually fades away till we are left with the two women silently continuing the conversation.*

*Music starts under as the lights fade to:**

Blackout.

---

*A licence to produce *A Brief History of Women* does not include a performance licence for any third-party or copyrighted music. Licensees should create an original composition or use music in the public domain. For further information, please see Music Use Note on page iii.

PART TWO

Kirkbridge Preparatory School 1945

CHARACTERS

MR SPATES – English & Geography, aged 37
DOCTOR WYNFORD WILLIAMS – headmaster, Classics, aged 50
MISS EVA MILLER – French, aged 40
MISS URSULA BROCK – History, aged 25
MR DESMOND KENNEDY – Sports, aged 30
MISS PHOEBE LONG – Maths, aged 45

TIME

The Fifth of November.

SETTING

Four separate areas denoting sections of the ground floor of Kirkbridge Preparatory School, including parts of the hall and main staircase and the terrace, both of which remain the same as before. The study is now the staffroom and the ballroom has been turned into the school gymnasium, which also serves as school assembly.

1945. Kirkbridge Preparatory School.

November fifth.

The manor has undergone a few changes since we last saw it. The hall and stairs are essentially the same, as is the terrace area.

The former ballroom has been converted into a gymnasium and the former study has been redesignated as the staffroom.

At the start, from the gymnasium comes the sound of young voices, mingled with one or two adult ones, singing a familiar hymn at the end of the school's morning assembly.*

Five members of the school staff are currently visible, standing with their backs to us facing offstage towards the unseen stage at the far end. These include: **MISS EVA MILLER**, *forty, French;* **MR DESMOND KENNEDY**, *thirty, Sports;* **MISS PHOEBE LONG**, *forty-five, Maths;* **MR ANTHONY SPATES**, *thirty-seven, English and Geography; and* **MISS URSULA BROCK**, *twenty-five, History. The latter pair have their hands secretly entwined, hidden behind their backs as they sing along with the others, with varying degrees of discordancy.*

Despite being indoors, the house is unheated and clearly very cold. Everyone is wearing varying degrees of

---

*A licence to produce *A Brief History of Women* does not include a performance licence for any third-party or copyrighted music. Licensees should create an original composition or use music in the public domain. For further information, please see Music Use Note on page iii.

*protection: overcoats, scarves, hats and, in some cases,
gloves.*

The hymn ends and the distant voice of the headmaster,
DOCTOR WYNFORD WILLIAMS – *MA Oxon, Classics* – *is
heard from the far end of the hall.*

WYNFORD *(offstage, distantly)* Now I appreciate it is cold but
we're doing all we can to have the boiler repaired as soon
as possible. I am informed that the engineer is expected
at any moment. In the meantime, you will be permitted
to wear outdoor clothing indoors and in the classrooms,
throughout the day, until this matter is resolved. Now, I
don't have to remind you that tonight is Guy Fawkes Night.
It has been brought to my attention that certain of you
have been commencing celebrations prematurely and have
been starting unauthorised bonfires in unsuitable places. I
would remind you that this is strictly forbidden. Any further
damage to school property and furniture will be severely
dealt with. I reiterate, there is to be only one bonfire, the
official school bonfire, this evening, supervised as usual by
Mr Kennedy. It will be held on the old back lawn, starting
promptly at six thirty, followed by a brief, I emphasise brief,
firework display. Let us pray. Dear Lord, open our eyes
that we may see only the good and the beautiful and turn
our heads constantly away from sin and ugliness. Amen.
Dismissed. I wish all of you a pleasant and productive day.

*A general shuffling as the assembly breaks up. In a
moment,* **WYNFORD** *strides into view. He is a busy,
bustling, slightly overweight Welshman, fifty.*

(as he passes his staff, without stopping) Mr Spates, a private
word, if I may?

He goes through the door onto the terrace. **SPATES** *trots
behind him obediently. As the door closes, the sounds
of the assembly are muted and replaced by birdsong
from the terrace.*

SPATES *(as he joins him)* Yes, Headmaster, you wanted a word?

WYNFORD Yes, Anthony. I thought we'd talk out here. It's a damn sight warmer than it is in there. My study's like a bloody icebox. Have you ever known a building to be so cold? It's like teaching in a mortuary.

SPATES It is very cold.

WYNFORD That confounded boiler, I can't tell you the times they've sent a man out to fix it. The kids are lighting fires in the dormitories, just to keep warm. We soon won't have a stick of furniture left in the building. Dear God! *(calming down slightly)* Now, yes. Mr Spates. Anthony. I wanted a word about fraternisation.

SPATES *(puzzled)* Fraternisation, Headmaster?

WYNFORD Between you – and another member of staff.

SPATES Ah, yes...

WYNFORD I couldn't help noticing lately that a friendship has been developing between you and our Miss Brock. An – amorous friendship, shall we say? Which I think, frankly, is somewhat unhealthy.

SPATES I'm sorry, I don't quite know what you mean. Unhealthy? Why unhealthy?

WYNFORD Our girls are – the children here are – they are, let's say, at a delicate stage of their development. Reaching an age when they are – rapidly approaching womanhood. If you follow me. I feel your example, yours and Miss Brock's is not a good one for them to follow. It might lead to – ideas, particularly in the sixth form. Set our students off on those undesirable twin paths of lust and concupiscence.

SPATES I really don't feel that either of us has done anything untoward –

WYNFORD Yes, I'm sure you haven't. It's just I would prefer it if you would keep it private. Strictly between yourselves and preferably behind closed doors. I have to say your clandestine handholding and furtive – illicit nuzzling has not gone unnoticed by other staff members and certain senior girls. It's disruptive and not helpful in facilitating the smooth, day-to-day running of the school. Point taken, I hope?

SPATES Yes indeed, point taken, Headmaster. We'll both try and be more – clandestine in future.

WYNFORD I'd be most grateful. I've no wish, you appreciate, to interfere in your personal...in your private... I hope you don't think that?

SPATES No, not at all...

WYNFORD It's just, you know, when it impinges – encroaches – it tends to infiltrate, if you follow...

SPATES Yes. I do see that. I'm sorry.

WYNFORD No, no, no...

SPATES It's just that Ursula – Miss Brock – is rather – demonstrative, at times, in her feelings...you know...

WYNFORD Yes. Yes. I was aware. She has – Miss Brock's inner feelings reside rather closer to the surface of her sleeve than most people's. Quite a woman of emotions. Quite – modern, wouldn't you say?

SPATES You could say that, yes...

WYNFORD Still she's coming on well. She's doing nicely. I think she has the makings of a fine teacher. Once she can get over her... I do detect small problems with class discipline, at present. I've found it necessary to intercede, to step in, on one or two occasions. But she'll learn, she'll learn eventually. Women today, eh? Very different from when I was young, I can tell you. In my day, you practically had to prise them open with an emotional crowbar, you know what I mean? Just to find out what they were thinking. Kept it all well hidden, under the surface. Like an iceberg. It was certainly true of Gwyneth – Mrs Williams, my late wife. Yes. *(he reflects)* Still, I digress. We're talking about you two, aren't we? Tell me, I don't mean to pry but are you both – are you both considering – making it more – putting it on a more formal footing? I'm only asking because it might just make things simpler for both of you.

SPATES You mean, are we thinking of getting engaged?

WYNFORD Just to make it more formal, you understand, more official.

SPATES Less clandestine? Well, personally, I'd like to take it a bit further. Things for me have certainly got to the stage when I'd like to consider making it more permanent. But I think Ursula still has reservations. Probably, I suspect, due to events in her past. She's reluctant to take it any further, just at present...

WYNFORD *(gravely)* Ah, yes. Quite so. Her late fiancé. Tragic. Very tragic. We lost many fine young men during that last conflict. A pilot, wasn't he? Shot down over Belgium in 1942, if I recall?

SPATES It was Holland. 1943. He was a navigator.

WYNFORD Tragic. Takes a lot of getting over. Brutally sudden. Mindless. Utterly mindless. Well we've inherited the residue, haven't we? A country depleted of young men and filled with emotionally damaged women. I mean frankly, Anthony, the reason I'm talking to you is I consider you, quite honestly, to be one of the few sane members I have on my staff. I consider you my scrum-half, Anthony. You're at the heart of things, a safe pair of hands. Reliable. Feeding out good clean ball. Lightweight but quick on your feet. You're invaluable to me. But if you'll take my advice, Anthony, and you know it's well intended, well intended...

SPATES Yes, certainly...

WYNFORD Extending the analogy, Anthony, don't for God's sake get yourself entangled in the scrum. Keep well back and wait for it to come to you. All right? Enough said?

SPATES *(totally lost)* Yes. Yes, thank you. Thank you very much, Headmaster.

WYNFORD Wynford. Please, Wynford. Or, if you prefer, Wyn. Anything but Winnie. I can't abide Winnie.

DESMOND KENNEDY comes jogging on in his running kit.

DES *(slightly breathless)* Excuse me, please...

WYNFORD All ready for this evening then, Desmond, are you?

DES Oh, yes. Ready to go, Headmaster...

He runs off.

WYNFORD *(to SPATES)* Healthy bastard, puts the rest of us to shame. You'll be staying for the bonfire later, Anthony, I take it?

SPATES Yes, we were planning to...

WYNFORD It's also going to feature Des's speciality. His homemade fireworks which, I must say, are usually pretty spectacular. Though I suspect somewhat illegal. God knows where he gets half his materials. Doubtless he has secret sources, being ex-Royal Artillery and all that.

SPATES I look forward to it. I've heard good things. It's ages since I've seen fireworks.

WYNFORD I promise, if it's up to his usual standard, you're in for a treat.

The school bell rings.

Ah! Here we go again. For whom the bell tolls. *The Iliad* and form 5C. A truly tempting combination. See you later, Anthony.

SPATES See you later, Headmaster. Wyn.

They both leave the terrace and go their separate ways.
At this point, time is condensed. A rapid montage of

*children's loud chatter as the staff move from area to
area at high speed, criss-crossing from room to room,
their voices calling for silence until everyone has gone
off to their various teaching destinations.*

A brief moment of silence.

*The school bell rings again for the morning break, and
the montage resumes again with children's voices and
staff imploring them to walk rather than run. As the
cacophony dies down again,* PHOEBE, DES *and* SPATES
are gathered in the staffroom for their coffee.

PHOEBE *(who clearly fancies him)* Are you ready for this evening,
then, Des?

DES Oh, yes. All ready to go.

PHOEBE Anything spectacular this year, have you?

DES Wait and see, you wait and see, Phoebe. I've got one, I call
it Magnesium Magnificence. It'll take your breath away,
Phoebe.

PHOEBE Wow! Sounds thrilling! *(to* SPATES*)* Wait till you
see Des's fireworks, Tony. All homemade. Makes them all
himself. You're in for a real treat.

SPATES Yes, I've heard rumours. I'm looking forward to it.

PHOEBE He's a pyrotechnical genius. No wonder we won the war.
It's thanks to people like Des. What have you got planned
for your big finish, then?

DES Aha! Just you wait and see.

PHOEBE Des always manages a big finish. Last year was
spectacular. The blaze of red, white and blue, very moving.
(sotto) Oh, God. Here it comes.

EVA MILLER *enters, surveys the room and, nodding to
the men, opts to sit at a distance from* PHOEBE. *The
women are evidently at loggerheads.*

PHOEBE We were just discussing the fireworks, Eva. I don't suppose you'll be staying for those this evening, will you?

EVA *(French-accented)* Yes, of course. Why ever should I not?

PHOEBE I didn't think you Germans went in for that sort of thing. Burning poor old Guy Fawkes? I thought you'd have been on his side?

EVA Sorry?

PHOEBE When you consider that for several years recently your Luftwaffe were doing their best trying to blow up our Houses of Parliament, I assumed you'd have been a rather keen supporter of Mr Fawkes?

EVA I don't know what you're talking about, Phoebe. You're speaking nonsense. For the millionth time I am not German, I am Swiss. Swiss!

PHOEBE Oh, yes of course. I do beg your pardon, Miss Muller, I keep forgetting.

EVA And my name is Miller! It is not Muller. Miller! Miller! Miller!

PHOEBE *(echoing her with a Nazi salute)* Ja! Ja! Ja!

EVA Oh, for goodness' sake! You stupid, disgusting racist woman. I am not sitting here looking at your abysmal unpleasant face any longer.

She rises and stamps out, angrily.

PHOEBE *laughs.*

DES Now, now, girls... *(shaking his head)* Dear, oh, dear!

SPATES I think Eva may be genuinely Swiss, Phoebe, you know.

PHOEBE Nonsense, she's a Kraut. A fifth columnist. Left behind from the war. She got abandoned by the Nazis, once she'd served her purpose and they dumped her. We had a list of those people at Bletchley. Dozens of them, everywhere, blowing up factories, destroying railway lines, all sorts of evil mischief…

SPATES She showed me her passport, she's genuinely a Swiss national.

PHOEBE And what was the name in her passport, may I ask?

SPATES Well, yes, granted, it was –

PHOEBE Muller. Eva Muller. Muller, not Miller. She's as German as liver sausage. Swiss indeed!

SPATES Yes but there are Swiss-Germans, as well. You can't just lump people –

PHOEBE *(angrily)* A German's a German! If I had my way I'd put her up against a wall and shoot her!

She stamps out.

A silence. **DES** *sighs heavily.*

DES You'll never convince her.

SPATES *shrugs.*

She's a fine one to talk, anyway. Keeps on about Bletchley. What they did at Bletchley. She never worked at Bletchley, not in a month of Sundays.

SPATES She didn't?

DES Nar. Women's Land Army. Spent the war flashing her tits in the hay with the farm boys, didn't she?

SPATES Did she?

DES I know someone who knew her. Recognised her. Nearest she's been to Bletchley is the bus stop at Milton Keynes. Hey, now she's gone, I'll let you into a secret. It's a rocket.

SPATES Sorry.

DES A rocket. I've made a rocket. A giant rocket. Wait till you see it. For my grand finale. Tonight.

SPATES *(at last comprehending)* Oh, I see. You mean for the firework display?

DES I'll let you in on that. By the way, you used to work on a farm and all?

SPATES I was brought up on one. It belonged to my parents.

DES That's how you came to miss the war, then, was it? Reserved occupation, right?

SPATES Right.

DES Are you a pacifist, then?

SPATES No.

DES A conchie?

SPATES No. Just a farmer's son.

DES *(looking at him)* Right. Cushy life, then? Milking cows.

SPATES *(staring back at him)* Not that cushy. Beats blowing people up, anyway. *(rising)* I'd better see what's happened to Ursula.

DES Yes, you do that, love's young dream.

> SPATES *goes into the hall, leaving* DES *alone in the staffroom.*

> SPATES *stands in the middle of the hall, looking around him for Ursula.*

SPATES Ursula...?

> *The school bell rings again, denoting the end of the break, and the time-jump sequence recurs once more.*

> *By the time it has finished with yet another school bell,* URSULA *and* SPATES *are sitting together on the terrace.*

> *A silence between them.*

Where did you get to at breaktime?

URSULA What?

SPATES This morning? At breaktime? I looked for you everywhere.

URSULA I went for a walk.

SPATES Ah.

URSULA Just round the grounds. Felt like some air.

SPATES Oh. Bad morning, then, was it?

URSULA Fairly bad. 5B again. I've got them all day.

SPATES Oh, dear. Not your favourites, are they?

URSULA I don't think it's deliberate. I think they just mean to tease, you know. I've got used to all the badger jokes, by now. You know, "Miss Brock, do badgers hibernate in winter? Because why are you still awake?" "Shouldn't you be asleep, Miss Brock?" But just lately they've started on us two.

SPATES *(startled)* Us?

URSULA They've – picked up that we're – seeing each other. So all the jokes have got rather – tasteless, you know. Sexual. And giggly. You know, young girls.

SPATES Oh. That's unfortunate. Especially in the light of the conversation I had this morning.

URSULA Conversation? What conversation?

SPATES With Pooh Bear. With Winnie. He was warning me about us not being too public about it. Asking we only did it behind closed doors, from now on.

URSULA We should be so fortunate! Even to find a door we could close in this place. Without risking someone walking in on us.

SPATES *(soothingly)* You're not to worry about it. We just need to be more discreet, in future.

URSULA How can we possibly be more discreet than we have been? We seldom touch each other, do we? We rarely get a chance to kiss, not properly. When all I really want to do is just to make love to you, Tony. I want to feel your hands all over my body. I want you to kiss me all over with your lips and your tongue, every part of me longs to be touched by you!

SPATES *(looking around nervously)* Yes... Yes...

URSULA *(aware of his discomfort)* I'm sorry, Tony. I know you hate me talking like this, I know it embarrasses you...

SPATES No, it's not that, it's not that I hate it, not at all. It's just that it tends to get me started as well... Believe me, I want to do all that to you. And more, darling. Much, much more. It's just this bloody place, it's impossible. Kids staring at you from the bushes. From under their desks. Staff peeking out of windows. It makes me feel we're constantly on show, like sideshow freaks. You know something. I don't think anyone else in this place actually likes each other, at all. Let alone loves each other. We're the only ones. It's extraordinary. They all seem to loathe each other.

URSULA *(thoughtfully)* You're right. It's this place. It's so beautiful, so idyllic, so tranquil and yet it's a prison. You're perfectly free to walk away, you know you are, and yet you can't move your feet. The only way out is to fly.

A pause.

(gazing at the sky) You know, he still visits me some nights. Just occasionally... In dreams. He sometimes appears, just to tell me it's all right. To reassure me, you know. It's all going to be all right, old girl.

SPATES This is Jimmy? Jimmy still visits you, does he?

URSULA Now and then. If I fall asleep, feeling especially lonely. He comes to comfort me. Isn't that lovely? Whispers to me, softly. The way he used to when he was alive. When we lay there – afterwards. You know. Whenever he was going on a mission the next day. Whenever I got so desperately frightened. Frightened for him, you know.

SPATES Yes. Well I'm here now, aren't I?

URSULA *(taking his hand, smiling at him)* Yes, you're here now, my darling. Oh, I do so love you, Anthony.

They appear to be on the point of kissing.

(pushing him away at the last moment) No, we mustn't, must we? Forbidden fruit. *Verboten.*

SPATES I really love you, too, Ursula.

URSULA Yes, I know you do. You know what he told me the other night? You know what he told me?

SPATES *(startled by this change of direction)* Jimmy, this was?

URSULA He told me I'd see him again.

SPATES Oh, yes. Up there, you mean? Probably in heaven?

URSULA No, not in heaven. Here. He'll come back to me here. In a blinding light.

SPATES Ah. That could be a bit awkward, couldn't it?

URSULA How do you mean?

SPATES Well, with the three of us? I'd still be here, wouldn't I?

URSULA Yes, I'm sure we could sort something out, couldn't we? Between us?

SPATES *(confused)* Possibly. I don't quite see how we could –

The school bell rings again to denote the end of the lunch break.

URSULA Oh, no! See you later, darling. 5B beckons.

URSULA, *kissing him lightly on the cheek, goes back into the house.*

SPATES *(shaking his head)* I don't see how there can possibly be three of us.

He also goes back into the house, and time once again accelerates as before. Staff reappear and disappear rapidly as they move during the afternoon, from place to place.

Children's chatter as previously.

The school bell rings again for the afternoon break and, once more, things are silent.

SPATES, **EVA**, **PHOEBE** *and* **DES** *are sitting in the staffroom, as far apart as they can get from each other.*

A long silence. They are all pointedly ignoring each other, involving themselves with some task, reading, marking essays or in **DES**'s *case, doodling a new firework.*

After a long moment, **WYNFORD** *enters from the hall.*

WYNFORD *(shattering the silence)* Sorry to interrupt things, everyone. Just to let you know I have placed Miss Brock's entire class in detention. I passed by just now and they were behaving like wild animals. I have told 5B they are to remain in their classroom and will not be permitted to attend either the bonfire or the fireworks. Carry on. Sorry to interrupt.

He walks away again.

The long silence continues.

In a moment, **URSULA** *comes from the hall, tearful, and enters the staffroom. She sits at a distance from* **SPATES**. *He tries vainly to catch her eye.*

In time the school bell rings again for the end of the afternoon break. Time speeds up again, and the staff reshuffle once more.

To end this, there is not the usual school bell but a great whoosh as the offstage bonfire is lit and a cry of offstage delight and cheers from the watching children and staff.

WYNFORD, *together with* URSULA *and* SPATES, *is now gathered on the terrace.*

(reacting) Hey!

URSULA *(with him)* Oooooh!

SPATES *(with them)* Bravo!

WYNFORD That's really rather spectacular, don't you think? *(calling)* Well done, Des! Even bigger and better than last year's, eh? You've certainly got the hang of it.

DES *backs into view, admiring his handiwork.*

DES Not bad! Not bad! Nice and dry this year. It caught nicely.

WYNFORD What have you got for the guy, then? Who's that sitting on the top?

DES Oh, it's just a bear.

WYNFORD A bear?

DES You know, a stuffed teddy bear.

WYNFORD A teddy bear? Good God, that's rather gruesome, isn't it? Setting fire to a teddy bear?

DES Don't blame me. Donated by 5B!

WYNFORD I consider that totally inappropriate. Some of these children have very disturbed minds. You can blame the war for that. So what can I see there on the launch pad, Des? That your latest creation, is it? Looks like a rocket?

DES That's your grand finale, that is.

SPATES It's very big.

URSULA Enormous!

WYNFORD Skyrocket, is it?

DES Sky's the limit. Take you halfway to Jupiter, that will. Wernher von Braun, eat your heart out, mate.

He moves away back to the bonfire.

WYNFORD We'll all look forward to that, Des, I'm sure. *(seeing someone by the bonfire, sharply)* Now, you girls keep well away from there! Stand well back, you stupid girl, that's no way to roast a potato, is it? You stand that close, you'll roast yourself as well. Stupid child. Miss Long, would you move them all back, please? Get them back behind the rope! No, no! Back! Back! Back! Oh, for God's sake...

He hurries off towards the bonfire.

SPATES *and* URSULA, *finding themselves alone, draw back into the shadows.*

URSULA This is cosy.

SPATES Very.

URSULA The first time I've been warm all day.

SPATES It's giving off a fair heat.

URSULA *(snuggling up to him)* We can imagine we're both sitting at home, our very own home, in front of a huge log fire, can't we?

SPATES Yes, we could. *(aware of her proximity)* Careful, now...

URSULA They can't see us.

SPATES They can.

URSULA They're all too busy looking at the bonfire...

SPATES ...Waiting for teddy to burn...

They laugh and watch for a little while. The bonfire gradually dies down, making it slightly darker.

URSULA *(suddenly overcome)* Oh, God, Tony, I love you so much. So, so much.

She turns and buries her face in his coat.

(muffled) So much! So much! I want you now, now...

SPATES *(a little alarmed)* Jesus, Ursula! *(trying to lever her away from him)* Ursula, darling! Don't do that!

URSULA *(still inside his coat)* Want you, love you, want you, love you, want you...!

SPATES Ursula, darling, please...

URSULA *continues unabated.*

DES *(offstage)* Right! Stand back, everybody. Here we go!

An expectant "Oooh" from the crowd.

URSULA *drops to her knees in front of* SPATES *and starts to fumble with the front of his trousers, trying to unfasten his belt.*

SPATES *(trying to prevent her)* Ursula, for God's sake, come on! Stop that! Darling! Stop it! No! No!

URSULA *(continuing)* ...Love you, want you, need you...

The scene momentarily brightens in colour thanks to a firework, ending with a bang. Another appreciative reaction from the crowd.

SPATES For God's sake, what the hell are you doing?

DES *(offstage)* Here we go then! Mind your eyes, everyone!

At this moment, SPATES's *trousers drop to his ankles. Instinctively, he turns his back to the crowd, also turning the kneeling* URSULA *with him, still clinging to his legs.*

DES's *penultimate firework, Magnesium Magnificence, illuminates the scene as if it were midday.*

(triumphantly) What about that, then?

A huge cheer and jeering laughter from the crowd.

WYNFORD *(a roar of incredulity, off)* Spates! What the hell are you doing?

SPATES *(appalled)* Oh, God!

URSULA *(emerging, suddenly aware of the brightness)* What's happening? What's happening?

She rises and stares up at the sky in wonderment.

(with an ecstatic cry) Oh! Oh! Oh, Jimmy! Jimmy!

DES *comes stamping on.*

DES *(furiously)* What the bloody hell are you playing at, you two? You realise you've just ruined Magnesium Magnificence with your sexual shenanigans!

WYNFORD *storms on.*

WYNFORD *(equally furious)* How dare you display such disgraceful, lewd, lascivious cavortings in front of the entire school! How dare you!

DES Right! We'll see about this, we'll see! Ruin this, then! Try ruining this!

He goes off determinedly.

URSULA continues to gaze heavenward, as if she's had a religious experience.

SPATES is still in a state of shock.

During the next, the sky darkens as Magnesium Magnificence loses power.

URSULA *(continuing to gaze up, murmuring)* Jimmy! ...Jimmy! ...Jimmy!

WYNFORD For Christ's sake, Spates, pull up your trousers, man, and cover up your equipment!

SPATES *(doing so)* I'm sorry, Headmaster...

WYNFORD *(shouting to the crowd)* You children, stop staring! Stop gawping, do you hear? There's nothing to see here, girls. *(attempting to shield* **SPATES** *from the eyes of the crowd)* Nothing at all! *(more quietly)* We will have further words about this, Spates! Strong words, you hear?

DES *(offstage)* Stand back, everyone, here goes the rocket to the moon!

An "Ooooh" from the expectant crowd.

DES *backs on again, a proud father watching the launch of his offspring.*

A faint crackling and a flickering glimmer as the rocket's fuse catches.

The others watch expectantly.

...She's going... Five... Four... Three... Two...

URSULA *(seizing her moment, rushing forward)* Wait! Wait! Wait for me! Wait...!

She runs off in the direction of the firework. The others react.

DES *(alarmed)* What are you doing? Keep clear! It's about to launch!

WYNFORD *(with him)* Miss Brock! What are you playing at, woman! Stay back! Stay back!

SPATES *(with them)* Ursula, for God's sake! Ursula, get away from it!

DES *(yelling in alarm)* Don't for God's sake touch it, woman! Don't touch it! It's just about to –

URSULA *(offstage)* Jimmy! Jimmy!

There is a loud whoosh as the large rocket takes off with a triumphal roar. Combined with this is the sound of **URSULA***'s voice ascending with it.*

(offstage) Jimmeeeeeeeeeeeeee!

*The others watch appalled as the rocket ascends a long
way. A momentary pause and then the final explosion as
it diffuses, first across the sky and then the countryside
below. They follow it with their eyes.*

A silence, both from those present and the offstage crowd.

DES *(finally, shaking his head)* There's no way she'll have
survived that, no way. She'll be spread over three counties...

He goes off, sadly.

SPATES *(stunned, deeply upset)* Oh, dear God! Ursula! Oh,
Ursula! Oh, my darling...

WYNFORD *(grimly)* Appalling. Quite appalling! Spates, you
are to hand in your notice and leave this school first thing
tomorrow, you hear?

SPATES Yes, Headmaster.

WYNFORD I plan to say a few chosen words at tomorrow's morning
assembly, followed by appropriate prayers, to which you'll
be welcome to attend as usual. But after that I want you out
straightaway. Is that understood?

SPATES Yes, Headmaster, quite understood.

WYNFORD What those children have been through this evening,
what they have experienced could possibly have scarred them
for life. Left them in deep traumatic shock. God knows what
I say to their parents, how I'm going to face them. *(wheeling
on **SPATES**, angrily)* I lay this entirely at your door, Spates!
You're entirely to blame! Entirely!

SPATES I don't think you can entirely blame me for it, Headmaster.
I mean, Miss Brock – Ursula, she did that quite spontaneously.
Of her own free will.

WYNFORD *(impatiently)* I'm not talking about the rocket, man,
not the rocket –

SPATES You're not?

WYNFORD I'm talking about your perverted sexual goings-on. What on earth's that going to do to them, do you imagine?

SPATES But they've just witnessed the sight of a human being exploding in mid-air, surely you can't compare that –?

WYNFORD Oh, they'll get over that. In time. They're resilient. No, I'm referring to the sex! The sex! That's unforgivable! Quite unforgivable!

He goes off.

(as he leaves) All right, everybody! That's the end of the celebrations! All over! Party's over! Juniors, to your dormitories! Well past your bedtime! Seniors, I want you all assembled in five minutes in the library for revision...

SPATES *(all alone again, sadly)* Oh, Ursula!

He, too, starts to leave slowly.

The school bell rings a final time, and the action speeds up again. The lights change to indicate the following morning. It is, once again, morning assembly.

The staff, with the exception of Ursula, are gathered as before. SPATES *has a suitcase. They stand while* WYNFORD, *offstage, addresses the school.*

WYNFORD *(offstage)* Good morning, everyone. I don't have to remind you that yesterday was a tragic moment in the history of Kirkbridge. We lost, through the most tragic series of accidents, a dearly loved, highly popular member of staff. I'm sure that we all carry fond memories of Miss Brock, of Ursula. Vivacious, fun-loving, and with always a kind word for everyone. Her smiling face and lively presence will be greatly missed. I know, speaking for all of us, she will not easily be forgotten. However, life must go on! Other events you witnessed last night I trust you will erase entirely from your minds. Those of you writing home regularly to your parents, I strongly urge you never to mention, in your letters, what you saw...

SPATES, in the midst of this, quietly picks up his suitcase and, virtually unseen, slips from the group. He crosses the hall, through the staffroom and onto the terrace. As he does so, WYNFORD's voice fades until SPATES is left alone with the morning birdsong. He steps off the terrace into the bright morning and gazes up at the sky as if searching for Ursula. He turns to take a final look back.

SPATES *(softly, to himself)* Goodbye. *(smiling, rather ruefully)* Goodbye. Again.

A moment. The bell rings and he makes a run for it as the lights fade to:

Blackout.

PART THREE

Kirkbridge Arts Centre 1965

CHARACTERS

ANTHONY SPATES – Arts Centre administrative director, aged 57
DENNIS DUNBAR – actor and director, Pendon Players, aged 50
PAT WRIGGLY – actress, Pendon Players, aged 40
JENNY TYLER – stage manager, Pendon Players, aged 22
RORY TUDOR – actor, Pendon Players, aged 24
GILLIAN DUNBAR – actress, Pendon Players, aged 45

TIME

A weekday evening in December.

SETTING

Four separate areas denoting sections of the ground floor of Kirkbridge Arts Centre, including parts of the hall and main staircase, which remain the same as before. The staffroom has now become the administrator's office, and the ballroom has been turned into a theatre, with its stage off at the far end. The terrace area has been glazed over, somewhat inexpensively, and serves as the theatre's green room area. Leading from this, further along the former terrace, are the offstage dressing rooms.

Kirkbridge Arts Centre.

December 1965. A weekday, early evening. The manor has again undergone a few changes over twenty years. While the hall area remains essentially the same, the former staffroom now serves as the office of the Centre's administrative director, **ANTHONY SPATES**.

The ballroom has now become a theatre, the raised stage of which is at the far end and therefore unseen. We have a view of the rear of its unraked auditorium, the seats of which are not yet in place.

The terrace area has been glazed over and is thus undercover and serves as the artists' green room of the theatre. Leading offstage from this are the dressing rooms.

Most of the activity appears initially to emanate from the stage, as there is a rehearsal in full flow for the local amateur Pendon Players' annual pantomime.

DENNIS DUNBAR, *the pantomime's director, leading man, leading everything else, backs into view now and then, as he directs something on the unseen stage. It is silent at present as the sound still follows* **SPATES**, *now aged fifty-seven, the Kirkbridge Arts Centre's director, who enters along the hall.* **PAT WRIGGLY**, *aged forty, a rather grand amateur actress, dressed in jeans and sweater as befits her role as principal boy, enters the green room from the dressing rooms. She knocks silently on the communicating door linking to the director's office.*

SPATES *goes into the office via the hall door.*

PAT *knocks again. This time, along with* SPATES, *we can hear it.*

SPATES *(calling)* Hallo?

PAT *enters the office.*

PAT Tony, is it at all possible, darling, to have the heating in the dressing rooms a tidge higher, do you think?

SPATES Yes, I'm sorry, Pat, I did get that message from Dennis. I've just been down to the basement and tweaked the thermostat a bit.

PAT If it could be the teeniest bit warmer, darling. It's just for the little ones, while they're rehearsing. Most of them are just in their pants and singlets. It's not so bad in the theatre, but their dressing room was icy, just now. Little blue legs, poor things.

SPATES Yes, it's particularly a problem with those dressing rooms, this time of year. All that glazing doesn't help, of course. I've been trying to persuade the council for ages to put in secondary glazing, but of course, that's way beyond the budget for a humble arts centre. As I say, I've just turned things up a notch. It might take a little while to come through. It's a good system but it tends to take its time.

The whole place is due for a major refurbish. I can't see that happening, though, not in our lifetime.

PAT *(dryly)* Yes, there always seems to be plenty of money for everything else, doesn't there. But never for the arts, for some reason.

SPATES I'll just have a check round, again. Excuse me...

He moves to the green room door and goes through it. PAT *follows him.*

Not too bad here, in the green room.

PAT No, it's at the far end there, in the dressing rooms.

SPATES Well, it should warm up soon, give it a minute or two. I'll just check the theatre.

He goes through the green room door into the theatre. PAT *follows him.*

We can now hear the sounds of the rehearsal from the far end, presumably from the stage, including a piano and the sound of children's feet. We're evidently at a dramatic moment in a Jack and the Beanstalk ballet number.

We hear DENNIS DUNBAR *directing his youthful corps de ballet as he moves to and fro, in and out of vision.*

PAT *and* SPATES *watch him.*

DENNIS *is a rather florid, slightly overweight man, aged fifty. The stage manager,* JENNY TYLER, *a rather intense girl aged twenty-two, holding the Jack and the Beanstalk prompt script, also backs on, mirroring his movements.*

DENNIS *(calling, over the piano)* ...And then we all group around the beanstalk – imagining that hat stand is our beautiful beanstalk – and we're all little tiny, green bean sprouts, ever so tiny – so make yourselves as tiny as you can, everyone – ever so small – that's good, Tina – lovely, Molly, my darling – and now we're all waiting for the rain – little tiny bean sprouts – thirstily waiting for the rain – no, Kevin, not baked beans, you stupid boy – don't be silly, now – Seriously! We must all take this very, very seriously – otherwise there's no point – and – listening for the rain – here comes the rain – listen for the piano – here it comes – now!

The piano ripples in an explosion of raindrops.

---

*A licence to produce *A Brief History of Women* does not include a performance licence for any third-party or copyrighted music. Licensees should create an original composition or use music in the public domain. For further information, please see Music Use Note on page iii.

DENNIS And – now we're all opening – opening up – bigger
and bigger bean sprouts – thanks to the rain, that lovely
refreshing rain, making you all – stretch – and grow, stretch
– and grow... Good, Martin, that's good! Try not to hit other
people, though... Find your spaces, no your own space,
Damien, not Sarah's, that's Sarah's space... And then, we
grow big enough, for the beanstalk to start to grow... *(to
himself)* Once the bloody thing arrives... Good! *(to* JENNY*)*
Where the hell is the beanstalk, Jenny? Any news?

JENNY Colin says he's well on with it...

DENNIS That's what he said last week...

JENNY And the week before...

DENNIS Every year, every single bloody year it's the same. Last
year it was Cinderella's coach – poor girl ended up having
to walk to the ball. Just so long as we get it for the dress
rehearsal, that's all. Otherwise it'll be Jack and his Invisible
Beanstalk...

JENNY Good title...

DENNIS *(calling)* All right! Thanks, kids. That's your lot. Home
for tea, now. You can have your baked beans now, Kevin.
Off you go! Thank you, well done, all. Same time tomorrow
please, those who can make it.

*General sounds as the children disperse to their dressing
rooms.*

(calling to the pianist) Thank you, Graham, mate! Well played!
Take a breather now. Five minutes. Then I want to work on
the first scene, including the song. As soon as anyone else
deigns to arrive.

PAT I'm here.

DENNIS *(seeing her for the first time)* Oh, hallo, there. Didn't
see you.

PAT That's all coming along nicely...

DENNIS Like pushing custard uphill…

PAT Once they're all in costume. Have they got their costumes yet?

JENNY Glynis is still finishing them…

DENNIS God, has she still not finished them?

JENNY When I last heard, she hadn't…

DENNIS What the hell's she been up to? She started them in August!

JENNY She had a big wedding, apparently…

DENNIS Not another bloody wedding! *(frustratedly)* It's a miracle, isn't it? A yearly miracle we ever get these things on at all?

PAT We always manage, somehow, don't we? Every year we say that, every year we manage, don't we? The show still goes on!

DENNIS I've a nasty feeling Jack and the Beanstalk might be a bridge too far. Listen, I'm just going to get my kit on…

PAT It's only a rehearsal.

DENNIS You know me, I need the basics. Never feels right, otherwise. Never feel quite in character, without the basics –

He starts to leave.

PAT Well, I'm not bothering –

DENNIS *(noticing* **SPATES***)* Ah, Tony, no chance of a bit more light on the stage, is there?

SPATES I'm afraid there's nothing rigged yet. There's working light you can have.

DENNIS We've already got that. Worse than useless. Stygian gloom up there. It's a panto, not Strindberg. Jenny, we'll have to rehearse down this end, then. I'm not groping around in the gloom. Set up down here, will you? *(as he goes)* Dear God, can life get any more difficult?

He goes off through the green room to the dressing rooms.

JENNY starts to move pieces of furniture from the other end and place them in a rudimentary set-up. A rocking chair, a stool, perhaps a small table.

PAT Do you need a hand, Jenny?

JENNY *(tersely)* I can manage...

PAT Only offering. *(dryly, to herself)* Ah, well, one can but offer...

There is no love lost between them, apparently. PAT starts to limber up for her rehearsal. SPATES stands and watches, feeling a bit redundant.

SPATES It seems warm enough in here, anyway. Yes. Right. I must get on.

He leaves the room and returns to the hall.

The others continue silently, with occasional brief exchanges between them.

SPATES is about to return to his office when GILLIAN DUNBAR enters hurriedly along the hall. She is forty-five, unassuming and pleasant-faced.

GILL *(rather breathless)* Am I late? Have they started, yet? I'm late, aren't I?

SPATES No, they're still – *(uncertain of precise term)* – they're still – getting things ready.

GILL I hate it, being late.

SPATES He's only just this minute sent the kids home.

GILL Dennis always tends to get so – tetchy when people are late. Has Anthea arrived yet? Any sign of Anthea?

SPATES Who? Oh, Anthea. No, I haven't seen her.

GILL Well, at least I'm here before her, that's a blessing. The traffic's appalling, it was a nightmare getting here. And then, when I get here, that car park's jam-packed...

SPATES I think that's the kids' parents picking them up. It should be emptying pretty shortly.

GILL I did find somewhere. Eventually.

SPATES If I'd known, you could have had my slot.

GILL Yes but don't you need it yourself?

SPATES No, most days I cycle in. Rarely use the car, these days.

GILL You cycle in?

SPATES I don't live far away.

GILL Must be cold, though, mustn't it? This time of year?

SPATES Freezing.

GILL Well, you're hardier than I am. I always mean to walk everywhere. Every day I say to myself, this is the day you're walking, Gillian, today you are *walking*! But I never do. I end up being in far too much of a hurry. Take the soft option. God, you'd think having worked at the hospital all those years, I'd know better. You see so many examples of people who just sit around all day, never taking any sort of exercise, all of them reaping the inevitable side effects. You think I'd have learnt, wouldn't you? *(aware she may be keeping him)* Sorry, I'll let you get on, you've masses to do, I'm sure. I think we're doing the first scene, Anthea and I are both in that. Our big number. See you later.

SPATES See you later. I'll tell Anthea you're here, if I see her.

GILL Thanks.

She goes into the ballroom.

SPATES *returns to his office.*

GILL *is seen speaking with* **JENNY**, *as a result of which she appears to get rather cross. This ends in* **GILL** *stamping out again and returning across the hall to the office.* **JENNY** *and* **PAT** *exchange a silent word or two, with*

JENNY *shrugging as if it wasn't her fault.* **GILL** *knocks briefly on the office door, then enters.*

GILL *(crossly)* Typical. That's just typical of that girl. Typical.

SPATES Who? Who do you mean?

GILL That – Jenny. Our new stage manager. She's just so – she just doesn't think, she never *thinks*, does she? It seems Anthea's had a fall. She called in earlier to say she'd slipped on the ice outside her front door. *Now* that girl tells me! I've driven all the way here for nothing. It's *typical* of her. I'm sure she's quite brilliant, when she's at university, studying for her whatever-it-is – sociology degree or whatever – but as a stage manager she's absolutely hopeless. I wouldn't mind but it's not the first time she's done this, either.

SPATES *(absorbing this outburst)* Well, at least you're here.

GILL Yes, that's the whole point! I'm here, Anthea isn't.

SPATES Can't you rehearse without her?

GILL *(rather irritably)* No, of course I can't rehearse without her. Not possibly. We're a team. We need to rehearse together. We can't possibly rehearse separately, we – oh, it's too difficult to explain. You wouldn't understand.

SPATES *(meekly)* Right.

GILL *(after a pause)* Sorry. I didn't mean to take it out on you. I'm sorry. It's hardly your fault. I'm so sorry. *(slight pause)* It's just that sort of thing makes me so ANGRY! *(calming down again)* Sorry.

SPATES OK.

GILL Seeing as I'm here, I suppose I might as well go and watch rehearsal. You coming? Want to watch a bit?

SPATES Won't I be in the way?

GILL *(leaving)* God, no. There's nothing Dennis likes more than an audience.

SPATES Well, if no one objects...

He follows **GILL** *out of the office and across the hall, where they enter the theatre where* **PAT** *and* **JENNY** *are waiting to start.*

GILL *and* **SPATES** *sit with them. A silence.*

Yes, certainly getting warmer in here...

DENNIS, *the star, makes his entrance. He is evidently playing the Dame. He wears a long, padded practice skirt and the traditional exaggerated bosom in the form of a vast padded bra. Graham, the pianist, plays an ironic piano fanfare.* **DENNIS** *bows extravagantly in response. The others applaud.*

DENNIS Thank you, I thank you. Settle down, boys and girls. We'll go from the top of the page, Pat, just before your entrance, darling. *(sitting in the rocking chair, in his Dame voice)* Oh, that boy! That boy! He'll be the death of me, will that Jack! One look at him, and he brings on my rheumatics something dreadful! Since my husband, Gabriel Grubstock, popped his clogs, we've been destitute! Destitute, boys and girls! Worse than that we're flat broke! Not a penny to our name. We've had to sell everything, everything! The washing machine, the cooker, the fridge, my shares in North Sea Gas. Now we've got to sell Daisy, our beloved cow Daisy! *(calling)* Jack! Jack! Come down here, boy! Get out of bed and come down at once, you idle sluggard! Jack!

PAT *(entering, yawning and stretching)* Whoarr! Yes, Mother, did you call? What do you want, Mother?

DENNIS Where have you been, boy?

PAT I've been in bed asleep, Mother.

---

*A licence to produce *A Brief History of Women* does not include a performance licence for any third-party or copyrighted music. Licensees should create an original composition or use music in the public domain. For further information, please see Music Use Note on page iii.

DENNIS Well, you're no use to me asleep, are you? I need you to go to market straightaway. It's market day and we need to sell Daisy.

PAT Oh, no! We can't sell Daisy, Mother, we can't!

DENNIS Oh, yes we can... *(turning and waving to an imagined audience)*

JENNY *(dully, as if by rote)* Oh, no, you can't...

DENNIS Oh, yes we can...

OTHERS *(variously)* Oh, no, you can't...

DENNIS *(in his normal voice)* And so on and so on – we keep that going, till they've had enough and we're bored to death with it. *(resuming)* Do as you're told, boy, you go straight to market and sell Daisy for the best price you can get. And don't you dare come home till you've got a big bag of silver. Off you go now. Leave me alone! I feel a song coming on.

PAT Yes, Mother.

She leaves the scene.

DENNIS If that boy brings home enough silver, why, I might even buy myself a new dress and a new set of stays, who knows?

The piano starts up an intro for his song.

I used to be quite a goer in my day, I'll have you know, boys and girls. Quite a little goer, yes...

YOU CAN TRY,
YOU CAN TRY,
TAKE COURAGE BOYS,
AND LOOK ME IN THE EYE!
IF YOU'RE LOOKING TO DRIVE ME CRAZY,
AND TO TICKLE MY WHOOPSYDAISY,
I'VE NEVER BEEN THAT KIND OF GIRL,
BUT YOU COULD TRY!
IF YOU FANCIES A BIT OF THIS, THEN YOU COULD TRY,
IF YOU FANCIES A BIT OF THAT, THEN DON'T BE SHY,

IF YOU FANCIES A BIT OF THIS, THAT LEADS TO A LITTLE KISS,
WHICH LEADS TO A BIT OF THE OTHER, THEN SO DO I!

YOU CAN TRY,
YOU CAN TRY,
COME CLOSER, LADS,
THERE'S NO NEED TO BE SHY!
IF YOU WANT TO CONFIRM THE RUMOURS
WHAT I'VE HIDDEN INSIDE MY BLOOMERS,
I'M NEVER ALLOWING THAT,
BUT YOU COULD TRY!
IF YOU FANCIES A BIT OF THIS, THEN YOU COULD TRY,
IF YOU FANCIES A BIT OF THAT, THEN DON'T BE SHY,
IF YOU FANCIES A BIT OF THIS, THAT LEADS TO A LITTLE KISS,
WHICH LEADS TO A BIT OF THE OTHER, THEN SO DO I!

*They applaud him rather more than he deserves, which
he acknowledges accordingly.*

He finally leaves the stage area.

JENNY *(dully, as before)* Cue forest front cloth. Cue lighting
change. Cue birdsong.

PAT *starts miming as she walks along the road, leading
the invisible Daisy.*

PAT Here I am, walking along the road, with Daisy, on my way
to market. Let me introduce you to Daisy, boys and girls.
Daisy, say hallo to the boys and girls. Oh, she's a little bit
shy, isn't she? You may have to shout to her. Everyone shout,
"Hallo Daisy!" Can you do that? All together, as loud as you
can. One... Two... Three... *(waving them in)* "Hallo, Daisy!"
We can do better than that, surely?

The others join in.

DENNIS Et cetera, et cetera, et cetera. Then the sequence with
the cow followed by comedy dance routine.

GILL *(standing)* Would you like me to stand in, Dennis?

DENNIS No point, dear, is there? Not till you've rehearsed it with Anthea, is there? Anyone heard how she is, by the way?

JENNY They've taken her up to Casualty, apparently.

GILL I'll give her a ring later.

DENNIS Well, we're buggered without her. No point in a two-legged cow, is there?

JENNY *(with a glance towards* **PAT***)* I know plenty of those.

  PAT *looks at her icily.*

GILL *(sitting down again, to* **SPATES***, sotto)* I'm the front legs, I do the front legs and the head. Of Daisy. Anthea's the back legs.

SPATES Oh, right.

DENNIS And – comedy dance finishes. Thunderous applause. And on to the scene with the merchant.

JENNY Cue in front cloth.

PAT Oh, my, I hate to do this, to sell our precious Daisy. Come on, Daisy, there's a good girl! But wait, boys and girls, look! There's someone coming this way! Who can this be, I wonder?

DENNIS And – cue the merchant – oh, where the bloody hell is he? Where's Rory?

JENNY Not here yet.

DENNIS Did you call him, Jenny? I take it he was called?

JENNY Yeah, I called him.

DENNIS *(getting agitated)* This is beyond a joke! Every week. Every single bloody week, it's the same!

GILL Now, calmly, Dennis. No point getting yourself into a state now, is there?

DENNIS I hope he turns up for the bloody performances, that's all I can say. Never here for rehearsal, is he? Never! We seem to spend our lives waiting for the man!

At this moment, **RORY TUDOR**, *aged twenty-four, sallow, rather sulky, with fashionably long hair, enters along the hall.*

GILL He's probably got held up, the traffic's terrible tonight, especially in the middle of town. It's this new late-night shopping they've introduced...

RORY *enters the ballroom.*

(relieved) Ah, yes! Here he is!

RORY *(nodding cursorily)* 'llo.

DENNIS *(heavily)* Well, hallo, good evening and welcome. Good of you to turn up, Rory, old boy. Thank you so much for gracing us with your presence.

RORY *(ignoring him, to* **JENNY***)* Got to me yet, have you?

JENNY Yes, bottom of page seven.

RORY *(pulling a dog-eared script from his pocket)* Right.

DENNIS *(to the others)* No word of apology, you notice. No "Sorry I'm late. So sorry to keep you hanging about, everybody. For wasting your bloody evening..."

RORY *(finding his place)* OK, I'm ready...

DENNIS *(shakes his head)* Unbelievable! *Unbelievable!*

PAT Can we get on, please? Some of us have been waiting some considerable time. We all have busy lives to get on with. *(to* **RORY***)* Are you ready then?

RORY Yes.

PAT *(back in character)* Good day to you, good sir!

RORY *(reading flatly)* Good day to you, young fellow.

PAT And who might you be, good sir?

RORY *(reading)* Why, I am a simple, strolling – ah – *(breaking off)* – Yeah, I think there's a misprint, it says piddler here.

Strolling piddler. That should read peddler, strolling peddler, shouldn't it?

DENNIS No, that's correct. That's perfectly correct. Strolling piddler.

RORY What's a piddler, then?

PAT It's a joke, dear, a joke.

RORY Oh, I see, a joke?

DENNIS *(slightly impatiently, sensing conflict)* Yes, it's a joke.

RORY Oh, right. OK. Ha-ha-ha, then.

DENNIS Provided you play it with the accent, it's a joke. You'll find it's funny.

RORY I don't see how it's particularly funny.

DENNIS *(angrily)* It's funny, because he can't pronounce peddler, that's why!

RORY You mean, he's got a speech impediment? We're making fun of a bloke with a speech impediment, is that it?

DENNIS No, he's not got a speech impediment, for Christ's sake –

RORY I'm not doing that. That's out of order.

PAT He's just got an accent, that's all. Play it with an accent.

RORY What sort of accent?

PAT He's a local yokel.

RORY A local yokel. Jesus Christ! Patronising or what?

DENNIS Oh, for God's sake! Give it here! Let me show you! I'll show you!

He snatches the script from **RORY***'s hands and elbows him aside.*

(to **PAT***)* Feed me the lines, darling. Let's show him, show him the sequence.

The following sequence is played at rapid speed. DENNIS *and* PAT *have evidently played it several times before over the years.*

(reading, in an exaggerated, rustic voice) Good day to you, young fellow.

PAT And who might you be, good sir?

DENNIS Why, I am a simple strolling piddler.

PAT A piddler?

DENNIS Yes, I'm a piddler.

PAT Don't you mean a peddler?

DENNIS That's what I said, a piddler.

PAT Oh, I see. What is it you do, then? As a piddler?

DENNIS I piddles things, don't I?

PAT You piddles things?

DENNIS Yes, I piddles things.

PAT What is it you are piddling at the moment, might I ask?

DENNIS At the moment, young fellow, I'm piddling beans.

PAT My goodness! That must be painful.

DENNIS No, not really, you see they're magic beans.

PAT I'm glad to hear it, for your sake!

DENNIS Would you care for me to piddle some for you now, young fellow?

PAT If you wouldn't mind.

DENNIS Not at all. My pleasure.

PAT Would you like me to turn my back?

DENNIS No need for that! Lo and behold! Hey, presto! Magic beans!

He mimes producing a handful of beans.

SPATES *and* GILL *applaud.*

RORY *and* JENNY *remain unimpressed.*

DENNIS *(to* RORY*)* There, you are. Something along those lines, all right? Brings the house down every time.

RORY You want me to say it like that?

DENNIS Yes, along those lines.

RORY I'm definitely not saying it like that.

DENNIS Why the hell not?

RORY Because I think that's offensive.

DENNIS Offensive? What the hell's offensive about that?

RORY Presumably this – peddler – he's meant to be a Traveller, right? And we're making fun of the way he talks. Making him look an idiot? I consider that deeply offensive. It's racially and socially prejudiced.

DENNIS What the hell are you talking about?

RORY You want me to take part in what amounts to verbal denigration of an underprivileged, persecuted minority? What sort of joke is that meant to be? Making fun of working people? Sneering at the way they talk?

DENNIS Oh, don't start all that bollocks, don't start all that!

RORY What bollocks?

DENNIS All that left-wing bollocks. This is a pantomime, man, not a bloody soapbox. If you want to start preaching, go out on the street corner and bore someone else rigid. I refuse to listen to this poppycock.

RORY No, that's the point, you never do listen, do you, your sort? Blind, deaf and dumb, aren't you?

DENNIS Listen, this is a sodding pantomime, for God's sake, for kids, to entertain children. A bit of innocent Christmas fun, you socialist arsehole.

RORY If you want to know what I think –

PAT No, none of us want to hear what you think, thank you –

RORY *(ignoring her)* If you want to know what I think, I think the story's symbolic. It's a symbol –

PAT Oh, what utter rubbish! Symbolic?

DENNIS Yes it is! It's a symbol! It's a symbolic fairy story of the struggle between good and evil. About a boy who swaps a cow for a handful of magic beans…

RORY …Which represents him finding the key to social advancement…

DENNIS …which overnight grow into a huge beanstalk…

RORY …denoting the social ladder that he's then forced to climb…

DENNIS …and living right at the top, he discovers a hungry, greedy giant…

RORY …embodying the spirit of capitalism, at its worst…

DENNIS …and Jack steals his gold, chops down the beanstalk and kills the giant. End of story. And they all live happily ever after.

RORY …social equality restored, system destroyed, death of capitalism! Long live the revolution! Hoo – fucking – ray!

JENNY Hear! Hear!

> **GILL** *begins to tug on* **SPATES***'s sleeve, indicating that they should leave. The two of them, during the next, slip away as unobtrusively as possible from the room.*
>
> *As they do so, the others engage in what develops into a full-blown argument between* **PAT** *and* **DENNIS** *on the one side and* **RORY** *and* **JENNY** *on the other.*

DENNIS What a load of pathetic, half-baked political cat's puke! What does that make the peddler, then, may I ask? Bloody Karl Marx?

RORY *(taking this very seriously)* Very possibly, possibly he could be...

JENNY Or maybe Lenin.

PAT Don't you start, girl, just shut up...

DENNIS So I take it you're refusing to play the scene as written?

RORY I certainly am, not unless it's rewritten. I'm not prepared to corrupt the minds of children by spouting fascist, Tory propaganda.

PAT Oh, do be quiet, you pompous little oaf! It's people like you who are responsible for bringing this country to its knees! I will remind you, this man fought a world war for the likes of you...

JENNY *(to the tune of "Land of Hope and Glory")* LA-DA-DEE-DA-DA-DEE-DA!

DENNIS You shut up as well, keep your nose out of this...!

SPATES finally closes the door on this. The argument continues silently in the theatre.

It rages on for a few moments, finally reaching a climax, causing the protagonists to scatter in various directions.

GILL and SPATES remain in the hall.

GILL Sorry. That was threatening to blow up for some weeks. That boy, he seems – I don't know if he does it deliberately – it's almost as if he does – he just winds my husband up. I think he knows Dennis has rather strong right-wing views and I think he goes out of his way to provoke him, rather. I've told Dennis not to let it get to him, but when it comes to his pantomimes he's terribly sensitive. He takes it all very personally, if anyone criticises them. He once punched the local critic outside Woolworths for giving him a bad review. He likes to control every aspect of things. He does everything, you see. Playing the lead, directing, casting, building the sets, making the props, the lighting – everything. He even tears the tickets. It takes him nearly a year to plan them. Come the end of January, he's already drawing up the ground plans for next year. Sketching ideas for the posters...

SPATES Yes, I gathered he's fairly – dedicated.

GILL Obsessive. I think that's the word you were looking for.

RORY *storms out of the theatre.*

DENNIS's *angry voice is heard momentarily as the door opens and closes.*

DENNIS *(as the door opens)* – And don't bother coming back, either, we can do without you, you talentless –

The door closes.

RORY *stamps past them along the hall, ignoring them both, and exits.*

GILL *(as* **RORY** *passes)* 'Night!

In the theatre, meantime, **JENNY** *starts to clear the set back to the far end.*

DENNIS *and* **PAT***, deep in silent conversation, go through the connecting door to the green room and then off into the dressing rooms.*

(after **RORY**'*s gone)* Oh, dear. I don't think he'll be back in a hurry, somehow. I almost feel sort of sorry for him, in a way. Everything seems such hard work for people like that, doesn't it? There's never any fun in life, for them, is there? I think we all need doses of fun, from time to time, don't we? Not too much. Not *all* the time. But we really do need to laugh occasionally. It's a sort of escape valve, isn't it, really, don't you think? A way of relieving the pressure. People like Rory, poor love, they're like one of those new pressure cookers. I don't think the poor boy's ever had a good laugh in his entire life. I've never even seen him smile, anyway. Well, only very rarely. He has a lovely smile, too,

when he bothers. Alters his whole face. Rather like yours
does. You're a bit the same.

SPATES *(startled)* Me?

GILL Yes, you've got a lovely smile, as well. When you want to.
But if you don't mind my saying so, I don't feel you smile
quite enough, either.

SPATES Don't I? Well, I must try a bit harder in future. I hope
I don't come over as gloomy as he does?

GILL No, you're not gloomy. Not exactly gloomy. But you do
seem a bit sad, though. As if your life hasn't taken you quite
where you wanted it to. You come over as a bit – disappointed
with everything, that's all.

SPATES *(considering this)* Perhaps. Maybe I am. Maybe. Very
astute of you.

GILL Anything you need to talk about?

SPATES *(a fractional hesitation)* Not really, no. Not now. Not
at this moment.

GILL *(a little flustered)* I'm so sorry. I didn't mean to be nosy.
I didn't want to give you that impression. Sorry.

SPATES *(aware he has been slightly abrupt)* Sorry.

GILL Well, any time you do, if I can ever do anything to help...
Just say the word, won't you?

SPATES Thanks. I may come back to you on that, sometime.
(smiling) You never know.

GILL *smiles back at him.*

SPATES, *suddenly embarrassed, attempts to change the
subject.*

Rory was right about one thing at least.

GILL How do you mean?

SPATES That was nothing like a local accent. The one your husband was doing for the peddler – pardon – for the piddler. I've never heard anyone with an accent like that. Not round here. I mean, I'm a local yokel, straight off the farm and I don't think I ever spoke like that.

GILL Well, you know. Pantomime. Artistic licence and all that.

In the theatre, JENNY, *meantime, under the last, has cleared all the furniture back to the far end and now returns in her coat and opens the door to the hall.*

(to JENNY*)* Oh, hello. Have we finished, then?

JENNY I have. Stuff it, I'm off.

GILL Are the others carrying on?

JENNY They're rehearsing their duet with Graham. 'Night.

She goes along the hall and exits through the front door.

GILL *(after her)* 'Night. Ah, well. *(to* SPATES*)* I guess that makes me redundant, too. They're hardly going to want half a cow, are they?

SPATES I think he might have given you a better part than that. Especially being the writer's wife. Something a bit more glamorous.

GILL *(with a slight shudder)* Oh, no! I'm very happy playing the cow. Nice short part, lots of laughs from the kids, and no one ever sees your face. Fine by me.

SPATES Is it always cows? Do you specialise in cows, then?

GILL Well, sometimes it's a horse. And one year, in Aladdin, we did try a camel. But that wasn't a huge success. We had terrible trouble with the hump, I recall. And, one year, in Dick Whittington, I did go solo and played the cat. Which I really quite enjoyed. Once I got over my nerves.

SPATES Do you have children?

GILL Yes, one. She's just turned sixteen. Old enough to be left alone. Mind you, she's at the age when she prefers to be left alone. Her name's Jo. Short for Jocasta, only she hates that. She's always just plain Jo.

SPATES She's never tempted to take part in the pantomimes?

GILL Jo? Lord no, she takes after me. I think she really wants to be a doctor, when she's older.

SPATES Are you a doctor, I didn't realise.

GILL No, a radiotherapist. At one time. Before Jo came along. I may go back to it. Providing I can retrain. Things have moved on a lot, since my day. No, Jo hates all this theatre stuff. Actually she's most terribly shy. She's at that age, you know, where she's become terribly self-conscious about her looks. It's a horrid phase to go through. Especially for a woman.

SPATES Did you go through it?

GILL God, yes. Who says I ever grew out of it? *(laughs)*

SPATES *(smiling)* Hence the urgent need to hide beneath animal skins? Most interesting!

GILL This is fast turning into a therapy session, all about me! How did we end up talking about me, for heaven's sake?

SPATES Well, I think you show great loyalty to your husband. Turning up week after week to play a cow.

GILL Yes, I suppose it's loyalty, in a way. I think it's also a way of trying to remind him of my existence. *(laughs)*

A slight pause.

They are aware of the slight change in tone.

SPATES Yes.

GILL Still, we don't want to go down that particular path, do we? *(more brightly)* So, you were brought up on a farm, you say? That must have been rather idyllic?

SPATES Bloody hard work. I was a muscle-bound kid.

GILL No, sorry, that sounded like some terrible townie, didn't it? All rolling in haystacks and pink-cheeked girls with churns of butter.

SPATES I wish...

GILL Have you always lived round here?

SPATES Apart from a couple of years when I was at university.

GILL Oh. Where were you?

SPATES Exeter. English degree. Just. Then I came straight back here to teach. For a brief while. In this very building, as a matter of fact. My whole life seems to have revolved around this place, one way or another. In the early days, I used to come up here when it was the big house when it belonged to the Kirkbridges. You know, Lord and Lady Kirkbridge, just to help out occasionally. On big occasions. They used to bring in the local help for their big do's. Grand balls and so on.

GILL *(gazing around)* Golly! It must have been grand. What were they like? Were they equally grand?

SPATES Not really. They were rather nice people, really. All things considered. Well, some of them were. They put me through university, actually. My family could never have afforded it, that's for sure.

GILL How do you mean, some sort of grant, you mean? A scholarship?

SPATES I think it was slightly more personal. One of the family took a shine to me, for some reason.

GILL *(smiling)* A woman? It must have been?

SPATES How do you know it was a woman?

GILL The tips of your ears have gone rather pink. They've pinkened. They've distinctly pinkened. Sorry, I'm embarrassing you, you clearly don't want to talk about it, sorry. What was it like coming back to teach here? It must have seemed odd?

SPATES Very odd.

GILL Was it a good school?

SPATES It was expensive.

GILL Yes, I'm sure. Was it any good, though?

SPATES Terrible. I was only here a short time. A couple of months.

GILL So briefly? What made you leave?

SPATES *(guardedly)* I left for – personal reasons.

GILL Another woman?

SPATES How did you –? *(clasping his hands to his ears)* Oh, God!

GILL One way or another, you've had quite a full life, haven't you? A house full of ghosts, then? No wonder you look slightly haunted. Like a character out of Edgar Allen Poe. Beware!

They laugh.

Listen, would you mind if I made a quick phone call?

SPATES Not at all, there's one in the office you can use...

GILL Only I think I should phone Anthea, to check how she is, poor love. It'll only be a quick one, I promise.

SPATES *(indicating the office door)* Help yourself. I'd better just check how much longer they're going to be. I need to know when to lock up.

GILL goes into the office and, locating the phone, starts on a silent call under the next.

SPATES, meanwhile, tentatively sticks his head round the door to the theatre. The pianist is practising part of the score.

The playing stops as SPATES appears.

(calling) Sorry to interrupt. Have they gone, do you know? Have the rest of them gone?

PIANIST'S VOICE *(offstage)* No, I think they're still rehearsing, somewhere.

SPATES Right, I'll hunt them out. Thanks. Sorry to interrupt.

The pianist resumes his practising.

It cuts off as SPATES *closes the door.*

He returns to the office via the hall.

GILL *(as the door opens, mid-call, cooing sympathetically)* …
Yes…yes…yes…no…you poor thing…yes… *(seeing* SPATES,
into phone) …Sorry, Anthea, just a tick… *(to* SPATES*)* Did
you find them?

SPATES *(sotto)* Not yet, still looking…

He moves to the door to the green room. GILL *resumes
her conversation.*

GILL *(into phone again)* Sorry, my love, back with you…yes…
carry on…yes…yes…oh…poor you…

*Her voice cuts off and she continues talking silently
as* SPATES *enters the green room and closes the door
behind him.*

SPATES *(calling tentatively)* Hallo… Anyone here…? Hallo…?
(moving towards the dressing rooms, louder) Hallo, anyone…?
Hallo!

DENNIS *emerges from the dressing room, hastily
fastening his dressing gown, beneath which it appears
he is wearing very little.*

DENNIS Hallo? *(seeing* SPATES*)* Yes, what is it?

SPATES Sorry.

DENNIS We were just – we're rehearsing in here. We're very
busy rehearsing!

SPATES I'm sorry. I didn't mean to interrupt. I'm so sorry…

PAT *enters behind* DENNIS.

She is also partially clad, having apparently dressed in a hurry. She has on his sweater and is, with both hands, holding up her costume breeches for Jack. In her haste, she has put these on back to front.

In the office, GILL *finishes her phone call. During the next, she looks with curiosity towards the door through which* SPATES *has just gone.*

PAT Who is it, darling, what are they –? *(seeing* SPATES*)* Oh, it's you! What do you want, Tony?

SPATES We were just wondering if you were going to be much longer?

PAT No, we're still rehearsing...

DENNIS We're still rehearsing...

SPATES Only I need to know what time to lock up, you see...

PAT As soon as we've finished rehearsing. You can lock up as soon as we've finished...

DENNIS ...As soon as we've finished. I've paid for the full evening, you know...

SPATES Yes I do appreciate that. Please carry on –

GILL *chooses this moment to enter through the office door.*

GILL *(as she enters)* I didn't realise you had this sneaky secret door into the – *(seeing* PAT *and* DENNIS*)* Oh! Hallo.

PAT Hallo.

DENNIS Hallo, there. Didn't realise you were still here, darling.

GILL *(smiling brightly)* Yes, I'm still here.

DENNIS We were just... We were just – just...

GILL Rehearsing. Well, practice makes perfect, doesn't it?

A slight pause.

SPATES *feels somewhat trapped in the middle of all this.*

PAT *(finally)* If you'll excuse me, I must go and get changed...

She turns to leave, revealing the front fastening of her breeches, currently around the back.

GILL Oh, Pat, love...

PAT *(startled, turning)* What?

GILL The next time you're rehearsing, dear, better make sure you don't have your breeches on back to front.

PAT grasps at her breeches and exits with as much dignity as she can muster.

DENNIS *(brightly, trying to fill a void)* Well, now! Tell you what, why don't we all go and have a drink across the road. Fancy a drink, anyone? Tony? Darling?

GILL No, not for me. I'm driving.

DENNIS Oh, right, of course. How about you, Tony? No? Well, I'll probably stop on, when we finish, have a quick one. I'll get a cab home, darling, don't worry. No need for you to – stick around.

GILL No, I don't think there's any need, is there? I think I'd feel slightly redundant...

She goes back into the office, closing the door behind her.

DENNIS and SPATES look at each other.

DENNIS *(in a jovial, manly, conspiratorial sort of way)* Shit! That's blown it, hasn't it? Shit! Shit! Shit!

He returns to the dressing room.

SPATES, after a second, returns to the office.

He looks at GILL.

SPATES *(feeling something needs to be said)* I – I don't –

GILL *(before he can say any more)* Apparently, poor Anthea, my friend Anthea, they think she may have fractured her hip. She might be laid up for some time. Which is a bit of a disaster. We're down to half a cow.

A silence. SPATES *stands there, feeling inadequate.*

There's no need to say anything, there really isn't. Not that there's anything you could possibly say, anyway.

SPATES No. There probably isn't, is there? Not possibly. In that case, I think I'd better start on my rounds, switching off, locking up, setting the alarms. It's quite a long business, place this size.

GILL It must be. Would you mind if I tagged along, kept you company? I mean, I think I could do with the company, as well…

SPATES Not at all, you're welcome. *(indicating the hall door)* After you, then.

They both go into the hall.

GILL Which way, now?

SPATES Through the ballroom – sorry, the theatre – still haven't got used to that in forty years – then up the old back stairs, what used to be the servants' stairs, right to the very top – the maids' bedrooms and the old nursery, now the life classrooms – and then we gradually work our way down again by way of the main staircase there, to the front door where the alarms are. It's quite a hike, I warn you.

GILL The sooner we start, then…

SPATES Follow on!

He leads them into the theatre.

The pianist is still practising.

The music stops, as they enter.

Sorry, me again. Are you planning to be much longer, only I was thinking of locking up?

PIANIST'S VOICE *(offstage)* No, I've more or less finished here, it's OK.

GILL *(calling)* Graham!

PIANIST'S VOICE *(offstage)* Hallo, Gill?

GILL *(calling)* Just before you go – do you have my music there? For our dance? Anthea's and mine?

PIANIST'S VOICE *(offstage)* The dance in scene one, you mean?

GILL *(calling)* Would you mind awfully playing it through for me, please? Couple of times? Would you mind?

PIANIST'S VOICE *(offstage)* No, not at all. Just a second. Try and find it...

GILL *(calling)* Thanks, so much! Owe you a drink! *(to* SPATES*)* Hold out both your hands – no, hold them out in front of you – like this – that's it. *(turning her back to him)* Now, bend over, arms out and grab hold of my waist –

SPATES *(bemused)* What are we doing?

GILL Come on! Grab my waist! That's it! Now, hold it. Hold it tightly. Tighter. Really tightly. That's better! That's good!

SPATES *(awkwardly bent over, holding on to her)* What the hell are we doing?

GILL And away we go! Thank you, Graham, and cue music!

*The pianist begins to play the music for the cow's dance.** GILL *starts to teach* SPATES *the simple steps, which he initially executes with difficulty and then, as they progress, slowly gaining in confidence.*

(commencing) And – left to the side – right to the side – left forward, left back – right forward – right back, and kick! etc, etc.

---

*A licence to produce *A Brief History of Women* does not include a performance licence for any third-party or copyrighted music. Licensees should create an original composition or use music in the public domain. For further information, please see Music Use Note on page iii.

SPATES What are we doing? I can't do this, I can't possibly do this...

GILL Yes, you can! You're doing fine! It's easy... You'll be my new partner, Tony, my new back legs! *(continuing to teach the dance)* And once again! And – left to the side – right to the side – left forward, left back – right forward – right back – and kick! That's it, you're getting it!

They practice some more.

(finally, triumphantly) Ladies and gentlemen, a cow is born!

They dance on. As the music plays and their confidence grows, one has the feeling, given time, that they might together make a very fine animal.

As they dance on, the lights fade to:

Blackout.

PART FOUR

Kirkbridge Manor Hotel 1985

CHARACTERS

ANTHONY SPATES – general manager, aged 77
GORDON – a hall porter, aged 50
CAROLINE SEABOURNE – a guest, aged 97
TILLY SEABOURNE-WATSON – a guest, aged 27
JIM SEABOURNE-WATSON – a guest, aged 30
RUBY JENSEN – a receptionist, aged 40

TIME

An early evening in summer.

SETTING

Four separate areas denoting sections of the ground floor of Kirkbridge Manor Hotel, including parts of the hall and main staircase, which remain the same as before. The staff administrator's office has now been transformed into a rather sumptuous disabled access room with three doors, the additional one (unused in the action) to an en-suite bathroom and the others to the hall and terrace as normal. The terrace has been rather expensively re-glazed with double sliding doors, two of which can be opened onto the gardens. The theatre space has also been transformed into the residents' lounge and bar, with the restaurant beyond.

Kirkbridge Manor Hotel.

Visible areas include the hall and stairs, which have much the same layout as previously; the terrace, which is still glazed over as before but in a considerably improved manner, including sliding doors from the bedroom and also leading to the garden beyond; linking to this is the former office, which has been transformed into a well-appointed ground floor (disabled access) bedroom.

At the other end of this is a third, newly installed door leading to an en-suite bathroom beyond. A third door opens, as usual, on to the hall.

The fourth area, previously the theatre, has been converted into the hotel's main residents' lounge and bar, leading, in turn, to the offstage dining room.

At the start, **RUBY***, one of the hotel's smart receptionists, enters along the hall. Simultaneously* **SPATES***, now aged seventy-seven, enters through the lounge. He is smartly dressed in a suit, shirt and tie and appears to be comparatively bright and sprightly from when we previously saw him.*

RUBY Oh, Mr Spates, I was in looking for you...

SPATES Sorry, Ruby, I was just having a word with Chef. Have they arrived?

RUBY They're checking in. Gordon's dealing with the luggage. I've confirmed with housekeeping that both their rooms are ready and made-up.

SPATES Splendid. I'll go and welcome them, then.

He straightens his tie and braces himself.

Before he can move, **TILLY SEABOURNE-WATSON,** *smartly dressed, aged twenty-seven, enters along the hall.*

SPATES *(seeing her)* Ah!

RUBY Oh, Mrs Seabourne-Watson, may I introduce our general manager, Anthony Spates.

TILLY Hallo there! Well, this is all rather splendid, isn't it?

SPATES Welcome to Kirkbridge Manor Hotel, Mrs Seabourne-Watson.

TILLY I have to say, I think you've done a wonderful job, it's magnificent. It must all be very much the same, surely, as it was originally?

SPATES More or less, more or less, yes. We've managed to sneak in one or two modern improvements. Like decent plumbing, proper central heating, air conditioning in the public rooms and so on. But I like to think we've had her restored to something of her former glory.

TILLY I think you must've done. You should have seen the look on my great-grandmother's face, the minute we stepped through that front door. You should have seen her eyes light up.

RUBY *(moving away, discreetly)* If you'll excuse me... I'll...

SPATES Yes, of course, thank you, Ruby.

RUBY *goes off down the hall.*

TILLY My husband's – Jim's just signing us all in. They'll be along in a minute.

SPATES It was a good journey, I trust?

TILLY Perfect. Couldn't have been better, couple of hours, more or less, door-to-door. With only the one stop on the way.

SPATES You made very good time, then. From Wimbledon, was it? Very good. Mind you, at this time, the roads are fairly quiet.

TILLY I think great-grandmama's a little tired, though. She may need to put her feet up, for an hour or two. It's a big adventure for her, this. She rarely leaves the house these days, unless she absolutely has to.

SPATES How old is your great-grandmother now, may I ask?

TILLY Great-grandmama? She'll be – let's see, now – ninety-eight in August.

SPATES *(genuinely surprised)* Good gracious! Ninety-eight? Good Lord.

TILLY Mind you, she's still amazingly lively. Mentally. No sign of her losing that yet, thank God. One or two occasional flights of fancy but nothing that doesn't happen to most of us...

SPATES *(laughing)* No, indeed...

TILLY Up till recently, she was quite physically active, as well, for her age. Played tennis well into her eighties. Still chasing around with the great-grandchildren, right up till a couple of years ago. Until her legs finally gave up on her and she needed the chair. But, these days, unsurprisingly, she does get terribly tired, quite quickly. As all the systems gradually begin to slow down, you know.

SPATES No, please, don't remind me, please!

TILLY Well, you appear to be doing all right, anyway. Must be quite a job, managing a place this size...

SPATES Oh, no, no, no! Not anymore, thank you. I retired a few years back. I'm only here temporarily.

TILLY I see, I thought your receptionist said –

SPATES I stand in occasionally for the regular manager, Peter Bonham, who's taking a well-earned holiday, at present. Whenever that happens, the management usually drag me out of retirement to fill in for him. But I actually gave up the job a good ten years back. But I still miss it, like to keep my hand in, now and then. It's no problem, we live locally.

TILLY You and your wife?

SPATES No, alas, I lost my wife a couple of years ago –

TILLY Oh, I'm sorry –

SPATES These days, I live with my stepdaughter, Jo, and her husband. They were kind enough to take me in, look after me. They're both doctors, so I seem to have fallen on my feet, somewhat. But I still like to come back, now and then, to see the old place.

TILLY Ruby was telling us, you and this house go back together quite a long way?

SPATES Oh, yes. Decades. I'm practically part of the woodwork.

TILLY Were you here in my great-grandmother's time?

SPATES Yes, I was.

TILLY Do you remember her? What was she like?

SPATES *(guardedly)* I really can't remember all that clearly. I wasn't – I only came up here from time to time to help out, you know, for special occasions. You understand in those days – I was strictly below stairs.

TILLY Oh, yes, of course. I understand she was quite a girl. Bit of a wild one, in her day.

SPATES Possibly. As I say, I really wasn't that – familiar – with the family –

TILLY No, quite. Things must've been very different in those days.

SPATES They were. They were, indeed.

A pause.

TILLY *moves to the lounge doorway.*

TILLY I don't know what's keeping them. *(slight pause)* Would you mind if I –? May I take a quick look?

SPATES Of course, by all means.

TILLY *steps inside the lounge.*

TILLY *(impressed)* Wow! What a room! *(looking up)* Just look at that ceiling! Quite a room!

SPATES It was originally twice this size. It used to be the ballroom.

TILLY *(looking more closely)* Oh yes, I see. It's been divided, hasn't it? You can see by the cornice there, can't you?

SPATES The management in their wisdom decided a room that size wasn't really practical, in this day and age. Although it was magnificent.

TILLY I'm sure it must have been. You must have nearly as many memories of this place as my great-grandmother has. You ought to get together, share your memories.

SPATES Yes. Maybe. I met my wife in here, you know. In this very room.

TILLY What, in the ballroom?

SPATES Twenty years ago.

TILLY What was it? At a dance?

SPATES A sort of dance, yes. We got married soon after that, anyway.

The others enter from along the hall.

Leading the way is RUBY, *carrying the room key. Following behind her is the ninety-seven-year-old* CAROLINE SEABOURNE, *formerly Lady Kirkbridge, now quite frail in her wheelchair, pushed by her great-grandson-in-law,* JIM SEABOURNE-WATSON, *thirty.*

Bringing up the rear is hall porter GORDON, *fifty, pushing a luggage cart with a solitary remaining suitcase on it.*

RUBY *(as she enters, to* JIM*)* ...And this will be Mrs Seabourne's room, right next door to yours. Nice and convenient for you.

TILLY Ah, here they are at last!

She and SPATES *move back into the hall.*

JIM Oh, this is splendid. Very convenient. *(speaking loudly to* CAROLINE*)* You're right next door to us, Great-grandmama, do you see?

TILLY Hallo there, all done and dusted, are we?

JIM Yes, all done. All signed and registered.

RUBY *has meanwhile opened up the room.*

GORDON *hovers in the hall with the remaining suitcase.*

RUBY Here we are. *(stepping aside to allow them in)* This is what we call our easy-access suite. It has the door here – *(demonstrating)* – leading onto your private terrace, which, as you can see, is double-glazed throughout, so it's nice and cosy even in winter. And on a day like today, you have the sliding double doors here, you see – *(demonstrating again)* – which open onto our new croquet lawn. So wheelchair access to the garden and the grounds is really not a problem. If your great-grandmother ever feels like a breath of fresh air, it's all very convenient for her.

JIM Oh, that's splendid. Absolutely splendid. *(to* CAROLINE *again)* You see that, Great-grandmama, you can take a turn round the grounds, if you feel like it.

RUBY *(moving back across the room)* And then, through here, you have the disabled bathroom… *(opening the door to this, to show them)* As you see, it has a double-width walk-in shower which can accommodate a wheelchair, plenty of grab rails and so on. It also links through, as I showed you just now, to your own room next door, so you'll have access to this bathroom, as well as your own, just in case of – just in case of sudden emergencies.

JIM *(peering around the bathroom door)* Oh, yes, that's splendid. Absolutely splendid. *(to* TILLY*)* They've thought of everything, darling. *(to* CAROLINE*)* See that, Great-grandmama? They've thought of everything, haven't they? You'll be all right here, won't you?

SPATES *(to* GORDON, *indicating the suitcase he is holding)* Just leave it there, Gordon.

GORDON *puts down the suitcase.*

RUBY *(moving to the door)* If there are no further questions, if you'll excuse me? Any problems, please call the front desk, we'll be only too happy to help.

JIM *(clumsily endeavouring to tip her)* Thank you so much for all your trouble. *(surreptitiously)* Here is a little – something. For your troubles.

RUBY *(accepting banknote he offers)* That's quite all right, sir, happy to be of service.

With a smooth precision the note passes straight from her hands and into GORDON's.

GORDON Thank you very much sir, too kind. Much obliged to you. Most generous.

He pockets the note, and he and RUBY *exit down the hall,* GORDON *now pushing his empty trolley.*

TILLY It's a beautiful room. Lovely and light.

SPATES It's one of our most recent ones. Only just been completed. In the dim distant days it was formerly the study.

TILLY Oh, the study, was it? *(to* JIM*)* Did you hear that, darling, in the old days this used to be the study. Presumably Great-grandpapa's study.

JIM The study? Good gracious! *(to* CAROLINE*)* This used to be the study, Great-grandmama. Can you remember it being the study? You remember that, do you?

CAROLINE *mumbles something.*

TILLY What was that? What's she saying?

JIM What was that, Great-grandmama?

CAROLINE *(indistinctly)* Never allowed in here. He never allowed us in here.

TILLY What's she saying, I didn't catch it?

JIM I think she said, she was never allowed in here. That can't be right, can it?

TILLY No, I think she must be getting it muddled up with the servants. The servants were probably never allowed in here. *(loudly to* **CAROLINE***)* It was surely the servants who weren't allowed in here, Great-grandmama! It was the servants!

> **CAROLINE** *shakes her head frustratedly.*

SPATES Well, you're certainly allowed in here now, Mrs Seabourne. From now on, this is your very own room. And you're welcome to come into it whenever you like. All right?

CAROLINE Thank you, so much.

TILLY *(to* **JIM***)* This is Mr Spates, the hotel manager, darling.

SPATES Anthony Spates, how do you do, Mr Seabourne-Watson?

JIM Hallo there. Thank you so much. This is all splendid. Quite splendid.

TILLY *(to* **CAROLINE***)* In the old days, Mr Spates used to work here, Great-grandmama. He was below stairs and he used to work here. Do you remember him, Great-grandmama? You remember Mr Spates, do you?

> **CAROLINE** *looks at* **SPATES** *blankly.*

No. She doesn't. Too long ago.

JIM There were probably dozens of servants, they must've had hundreds of them in those days.

TILLY Stand a little closer to her, Mr Spates, see if she recognises you.

SPATES *moves closer to the wheelchair.*

(to CAROLINE *again)* This is Mr Spates, Great-grandmama. Anthony Spates? Remember Anthony, do you? *(waits)* No.

JIM No.

They are both about to give up when CAROLINE *begins to give the beginnings of a smile. Still staring at* SPATES, *she very slowly and awkwardly lifts her arm towards his face.*

TILLY My God, look at that... I think she actually remembers him.

JIM She actually remembers, yes.

They watch with bated breath as CAROLINE*'s hand reaches out to* SPATES*'s face. He bends slightly towards her so she can reach him. Finally, she touches him.*

TILLY Isn't that amazing? Isn't that just so incredible? I think she actually remembers you, Mr Spates. She genuinely remembers.

JIM Remarkable. When you think how many servants they must've had...

CAROLINE *(softly)* His first kiss. I gave him his first kiss.

TILLY What's she saying?

SPATES Nothing.

JIM I can't hear. Something about a kiss, I think.

CAROLINE *(softly)* I gave this boy his very first kiss...

TILLY She says she gave him his very first kiss...

JIM Oh, no, that can't be right, can it? His very first kiss?

TILLY No, that can't be right. She's drifted. She's drifting again.

JIM She's probably overtired. Long journey.

TILLY *(to* SPATES*)* I'm terribly sorry. She's obviously mistaken you for someone else. She does get a little confused, now and then. *(to* CAROLINE*)* We'll get you into bed in a minute, Great-grandmama. Let you have a nice lie down. Then we'll all have some tea. All right? Wait there! Darling, I need to go next door to unpack a few things, her medication and so on. Wait there! Won't be a moment, Great-grandmama! Darling, would you give me a hand with the big heavy case?

JIM Oh, yes, sure.

They make to leave.

TILLY Would you mind most awfully keeping her company for a moment, Anthony?

SPATES Not at all.

JIM *(jovially)* I think she's taken a shine to you, old boy. You may be onto a good thing there. *(laughs)*

TILLY *(giggling)* Jim! Honestly! What a thing to say! It's my great-grandmama!

She and JIM *leave the room and go along the hall to their own room.*

CAROLINE *has remained staring at* SPATES.

CAROLINE Your first kiss. Your first proper kiss, wasn't it?

SPATES It was. My very first.

CAROLINE Not the last one, I bet.

SPATES No, it wasn't.

CAROLINE You naughty boy.

She rocks her wheelchair, as if wanting to move.

SPATES What's the matter? What is it?

CAROLINE The garden. Take me out in the garden.

SPATES Into the garden? What do you want to go into the garden for?

CAROLINE The garden. I want to be in the garden...

SPATES All right. *(starting to push her through the terrace door)* We'll have to be quick, though. You ought to be having a lie down, you heard what your great-granddaughter said. You'll get me into trouble. They'll think I've abducted you. Just a tick.

He opens the sliding doors from the terrace to the garden itself. Birdsong.

There! Now, we can't go far. We're not going too far, do you hear?

They go a little way into the garden, and suddenly **CAROLINE** *indicates that he should stop.*

All right? Far enough? Want to go back now? Want to go back in, do you?

CAROLINE Want to look at the house. I need to look at the house.

SPATES OK. You want to look at the house? OK.

He turns her round so they face the house.

CAROLINE They never forget, you know, they never forget you.

SPATES Who? Who never forgets you?

CAROLINE Houses. They never forget you. They always remember you.

SPATES *(humouring her slightly)* Do they? That's nice. That's a nice thought.

CAROLINE Listen. Can you hear it?

SPATES Hear what?

CAROLINE It's talking to us, can you hear? Can you hear it? Listen...

SPATES *(straining to hear)* No, I'm afraid I can't... I can't...no...

CAROLINE *reaches up with her hand and gropes behind her, searching for his. He takes her hand and holds it.*

Faintly, from the direction of what used to be the ballroom, the sound of the piano music for Daisy the cow's dance from twenty years ago.

Oh, yes, now I can hear it. I can hear it now...

As it grows louder, they both listen, though whether both are hearing the same music is open to question.

As they continue to stand there, the lights fade to:

Blackout.

End of Play

---

*A licence to produce *A Brief History of Women* does not include a performance licence for any third-party or copyrighted music. Licensees should create an original composition or use music in the public domain. For further information, please see Music Use Note on page iii.

FURNITURE & PROPS

Two ballroom chairs

Study desk and two chairs

Silver tray

Cocktail

Empty drinks glasses

Two glasses of brandy

Varying overcoats, scarves, hats, gloves

Coffees

Books and stationery in staffroom – books, notebooks and pens/pencils for marking or doodling

Suitcase

Jack and the Beanstalk prompt script

Rocking chair

Stool

Small table

Padded practise skirt

Exaggerated padded bra

Dog-eared script

Coat

Telephone

Dressing gown

Costume breeches

Bed

Room key

Wheelchair

Luggage cart

Suitcase

Banknote

SOUND EFFECTS

General note: when Spates moves between rooms, we only hear what he hears at that time.

Part One

The sound of bar activity and muffled sound of a small twenties dance band.   p1

The music increases in volume, along with the sounds of general activity and chatter.   p1

The sounds of the ballroom reduce sharply, replaced by the hall sounds.   p5

Bar noises return.   p8

Ballroom music increases in volume.   p8

The band is still playing.   p19

Music starts under.   p28

Part Two

The sound of young voices and one or two adult ones, singing a familiar hymn.   p31

The hymn ends.   p31

General shuffling as the assembly breaks up.   p32

The sounds of the assembly are muted and replaced by birdsong.   p32

The school bell rings.   p36

Rapid montage – children's loud chatter, teachers' voices calling for silence.   p36

A brief moment of silence before the school bell rings again and the montage resumes with staff imploring children to walk rather than run.   p36

The cacophony dies down again.   p37

The school bell rings again and the time-jump sequence recurs.   p40

The sequence finishes with another school bell.   p40

The school bell rings again.   p43

Children's chatter as previously.   p43

The school bell rings for the afternoon break and, once more, things are silent.   p43

The school bell rings again for the end of afternoon break. p43

Time speeds up again (sound montage). p44

The montage ends as a great whoosh of the offstage bonfire being lit
    is heard. p44

A cry of offstage delight and cheers from watching children and staff. p44

An expectant "oooh" from the crowd. p46

A firework, ending with a bang. p47

Another appreciative reaction from the crowd. p47

Magnesium Magnificence firework followed by a huge cheer and
    jeering laughter. p47

An "oooh" from the expectant crowd. p48

A faint crackling as the rocket's fuse catches. p48

A loud whoosh as the large rocket takes off with a triumphal roar. p49

A momentary pause and then the final explosion. p49

The school bell rings a final time and the action speeds up again. p51

Morning birdsong. **p51**

Part Three

The sounds of the rehearsal, including a piano and children's feet. p57

The piano ripples in an explosion of raindrops. p57

General sounds as the children disperse to their dressing rooms. p58

An ironic piano fanfare. p63

The piano starts up an intro for Dennis' song. p64

Door opens as Dennis is heard from offstage. p72

The door closes. p72

The pianist is practising part of the score. p78

The playing stops as Spates appears. p78

The pianist resumes his practising. p79

The piano cuts off as Spates closes the door. p79

The pianist is still practicing. p82

Music stops as they enter the theatre. p82

Pianist begins to play the cow's dance. p83

They dance on until the end (music fades). p84

Part Four

Birdsong.   p97

Faintly, the sound of the piano music for the cow dance.   p98

The music grows louder.   p98

LIGHTING

Part One

Lights fade up.   p1

Blackout.   p28

Part Two

Lights fade up.   p31

The offstage bonfire is lit.   p44

The bonfire gradually dies down, making it slightly darker.   p46

The scene momentarily brightens in colour thanks to a firework.   p47

Magnesium Magnificence firework illuminates the scene as if it were midday.   p47

The sky darkens as Magnesium Magnificence loses power.   p48

A flickering glimmer as the rocket's fuse catches.   p48

The *(offstage)* rocket diffuses, first across the sky and then the countryside below.   p49

The lights change to indicate the following morning.   p51

Lights fade to blackout.   p52

Part Three

Lights fade up.   p55

Lights fade to blackout.   p84

Part Four

Lights fade up.   p87

Lights fade to blackout.   p98

Other plays by ALAN AYCKBOURN
published and licensed by Concord Theatricals

Absent Friends

Arrivals and Departures

Awaking Beauty

Bedroom Farce

Better Off Dead

Body Language

Callisto 5

The Champion of Paribanou

A Chorus of Disapproval

Comic Potential

Communicating Doors

Confusions

Consuming Passions

A Cut in the Rates

Dreams from a Summer House

Drowning on Dry Land

Ernie's Incredible Illucinations

Family Circles

Farcicals

FlatSpin

GamePlan

Gizmo

Haunting Julia

Henceforward...

Hero's Welcome

House & Garden

How the Other Half Loves

If I Were You

Improbable Fiction

Intimate Exchanges, Volume I

Intimate Exchanges, Volume II

It Could Be Any One of Us

Joking Apart

Just Between Ourselves

Life and Beth

Life of Riley

Living Together

Man of the Moment

Me, Myself and I

Mixed Doubles

Mr A's Amazing Maze Plays

Mr Whatnot

My Very Own Story

My Wonderful Day

Neighbourhood Watch

No Knowing

The Norman Conquests: Table Manners; Living Together;
Round and Round the Garden

Private Fears in Public Places

Relatively Speaking

The Revengers' Comedies

RolePlay

Roundelay

Season's Greetings

Sisterly Feelings

A Small Family Business

Snake in the Grass

Suburban Strains

Sugar Daddies

Taking Steps

Ten Times Table

Things We Do for Love

This Is Where We Came In

Time and Time Again

Time of My Life

Tons of Money (revised)

Way Upstream

Wildest Dreams

Wolf at the Door

Woman in Mind

A Word from Our Sponsor

Other plays by ALAN AYCKBOURN
licensed by Concord Theatricals

The Boy Who Fell Into a Book

Invisible Friends

The Jollies

Orvin – Champion of Champions

Surprises

Whenever

FIND PERFECT PLAYS TO PERFORM AT
www.concordtheatricals.co.uk
www.concordtheatricals.co.uk

ABOUT THE AUTHOR

Alan Ayckbourn has worked in theatre as a playwright and director for over fifty years, rarely if ever tempted by television or film, which perhaps explains why he continues to be so prolific. To date he has written more than eighty plays, many one-act plays and a large amount of work for the younger audience. His work has been translated into over thirty-five languages, is performed on stage and television throughout the world and has won countless awards.

Major successes include: *Relatively Speaking*, *How the Other Half Loves*, *Absurd Person Singular*, *Bedroom Farce*, *A Chorus of Disapproval* and *The Norman Conquests*. In recent years, there have been revivals of *Season's Greetings* and *A Small Family Business* at the National Theatre; in the West End *Absent Friends*, *A Chorus of Disapproval*, *Relatively Speaking* and *How the Other Half Loves*; and at Chichester Festival Theatre, major revivals of *Way Upstream* in 2015 and *The Norman Conquests* in 2017. 2019 also saw the publication of his first work of prose fiction, *The Divide*.

Artistic director of the Stephen Joseph Theatre from 1972-2009, where almost all his plays have been first staged, he continues to direct his latest new work there. He was honoured to be appointed the SJT's first Director Emeritus during 2018. He has been inducted into the American Theater Hall of Fame, received the 2010 Critics' Circle Award for Services to the Arts and became the first British playwright to receive both Olivier and Tony Special Lifetime Achievement Awards. He was knighted in 1997 for services to the theatre.

Ingram Content Group UK Ltd.
Milton Keynes UK
UKHW020933100323
418370UK00015B/1084